CHARTRES

Other cathedrals of the Christian world have not known how to say so many things, nor how to say them in such splendid order. There is nothing in Italy, Spain or England to be compared with Chartres. Chartres is the very spirit of the middle ages made manifest.

EMILE MÂLE

CHARTRES

THE MASONS WHO BUILT A LEGEND

John James

Routledge & Kegan Paul
London, Boston, Melbourne and Henley

First published in 1982
by Routledge & Kegan Paul Ltd
39 Store Street, London WC1E 7DD,
9 Park Street, Boston, Mass. 02108, USA,
296 Beaconsfield Parade, Middle Park,
Melbourne, 3206, Australia, and
Broadway House, Newtown Road,
Henley-on-Thames, Oxon RG9 1EN
Set in 11/14 pt Ehrhardt
and printed in Great Britain by
BAS Printers Limited

Library of Congress Cataloging in Publication Data

James, John, 1931–
Chartres, the masons who built a legend.

Bibliography: p.
Includes index.
1. Cathédrale de Chartres.   I. Title.
BX4629.C47C374   726'.6'094451   81-14370

ISBN 0-7100-0886-4   AACR2

THIS BOOK BELONGS TO HILARY,
who lovingly nurtured us all while it was evolving, and
to our three girls, Cassandra, Rebecca and Emily,
who made our lives a joy during those years

CONTENTS

I

THE CATHEDRAL

OF THE MULTITUDE of cathedrals and churches left to us from the middle ages, the most impressive is the especial home of Our Lady at Chartres. It is today almost exactly as men saw it seven hundred years ago, with most of its original stained glass and much of its sculpture. Only the choir stalls have gone, and with them the gold and brass and precious stones that once made the cathedral such a radiant spectacle. It is built of a hard, durable, purplish-grey limestone. Repairs have been few and, greatest good fortune of all, neither the vainglorious improvers of the later middle ages nor the smug restorers of the nineteenth century have affected it. By comparison, Notre-Dame in Paris is surrounded by chapels of a later style added to and obliterating the original walls; Soissons and Reims were both heavily knocked about by war; and Durham had up to 100 mm stripped off its entire exterior to smarten up the worn sandstone. Viollet-le-Duc, Wyat and other restorers, though they preserved buildings that might otherwise have tumbled down, altered them to what they thought the mediaeval architects should have built, rather than to what they did build.

But Chartres is one of the few to have been preserved almost intact. It gives us a tantalising glimpse into what much of Christian Europe must have been like in those days. About the year 1200 over a dozen cathedrals like Chartres were being built in the region around Paris, as well as some four hundred churches, thousands of abbeys and bridges and town walls and houses. It was one of the greatest ages of building the world has ever seen. For four generations a frantic and insatiable urge to construct consumed the riches of France. Some time during the 1230s, when Chartres was almost complete, the fever died away. Work slowed down and buildings that had been finished in forty years now took centuries. The religious enthusiasm generated during the twelfth century was exhausted.

1 The huge bulk of the cathedral rises over the town, dominating its low buildings much as it did in the middle ages.

The great age of pilgrimages passed, too, and the many thousands who had once flowed through Chartres on their way to the tomb of Christ's brother James in Compostela were reduced to a trickle, and took other roads. The region was by-passed by history and by war, as well as by prosperity. The good wines which came from the Beauce in

2 South elevation of the cathedral.

the thirteenth century declined in quality. The cloth-weavers who had done well on the pilgrim trade found themselves too far from the new markets to the north and east of Paris, and without the climatic advantages of other regions. Gradually Chartres receded into a rural backwater, while the great events that excited the rest of France happily left it alone. The region remained a reasonably prosperous one, with its rich wheatfields and silver mines, but, lacking both merchant princes and aristocratic grandees, there was neither the money nor the stimulation to change the cathedral. How fortunate for us. Because of that we can experience it as it was in 'the good days of the sainted King Louis', as they used to say.

What we see today is substantially the work of one generation. There have been few changes since then: a small chapel was added to one bay of the nave, the organ was moved up from the aisles into the clerestory and the old narthex was pulled down. Later the beautiful stalls and *jubé* were replaced with the present screen, and in the nineteenth century the roof caught fire and was rebuilt in a cast iron and copper structure that is quite remarkable in its own right. Some of the stained glass has been lost through the natural attrition of a delicate and perishable material, and a few of the sculptured figures were destroyed during the revolution. But that is all.

What we see and what stirs thousands of pilgrims and millions of tourists each year is essentially the same building that excited our ancestors. Historians have been just as moved as anyone else, and there are more theories about its history and the meanings that may have been written into it than about any other mediaeval building.

Chartres seems to pose as many riddles as the Sphinx. The books and theories on it are endless. As the most authentic surviving example of the spirit of 1200, which was itself one of the most spiritual periods of European history, it has naturally excited people of all persuasions. There is no other European building that appeals so deeply to scholarship and to fantasy, to the researcher and the devout. How did this happen? What sort of people were these mediaeval builders that they could impress themselves across so many centuries? And how indeed was a work of such genius designed?

Little in fact is known about the builders. A name crops up here and there, and a few comments that assure us that they were no more anonymous than we are. We read of the masters sitting at the high table with their clients, the lords and bishops. We hear of others

being the friends of kings, and of their hawking and their wealth. Occasionally in later centuries they had their portraits carved and set alongside those of the donors themselves. But for the first half of the middle ages we know next to nothing of the men who created Gothic architecture. One of the world's great art styles would seem to have come into being without leaving a trace of the people who made it.

We know that this building lies over the ruins of earlier ones which had been variously destroyed by fire and war. In 1020 they replaced a smaller church with one almost as large as the present cathedral, and in the 1130s a couple of bays were added to the western end, with a narthex and two towers, and between them the famous sculpture of the Royal Portal. This end survived the dreadful fire of 1194, and in the rebuilding that followed nearly all trace of the eleventh-century structure was lost, save the crypt. The new building was placed over this crypt and backed against the western towers, and except for these remnants the cathedral is entirely a product of the years around 1200.

The ideas created in the rebuilding formed a canon that others followed for centuries to come. It set new standards that were so successful that their influence can be felt in every country where Gothic is found. The interior was simplified into three storeys, while the outside was complicated with flyers and the heavy buttresses needed to support them. The tentative use of shafts found elsewhere was unified so that the visual mass of the vaults, which had earlier been gathered into the ribs, was now brought all the way to the ground through appropriate bundles of columns tied to the walls and piers. From inside and outside the energy of the building was not just implicit, but could be seen to be flowing and pulsing through it.

In one sense it is true to say that at Chartres was created the first and, probably until our own day, the only architecture to enhance structure above that of form and to create spaces held together in a dynamic equilibrium, rather than in static rest. Though this may not seem true in some particulars, just compare Gothic to the profoundly traditional architecture of Egypt or Assyria, or even of Greece and Rome. Those spaces have the regular density of a forest, and their styles remained within a stable tradition in which there were slow developments over centuries which enriched but never transformed the dominant motifs. The architecture of northern Europe continued this solid-wall tradition up to the twelfth century, but by the end of the century a revolution had occurred.

3 The first unified interior that inaugurated the style we call Gothic, with its three-storey elevation, its shafts that continue from the floor to the vault, and its enormous areas of glass. Chartres set the standards for many to follow.

4 The mass of the building was expressed as forces which flowed through wall and down arches and buttresses to the ground. The flyers which intersected one another where the choir meets the southern transept are one of the most exciting demonstrations of this energy to be found in Europe.

These years are renowned for the range of ideas, the proliferation of new and highly experimental forms, and the daring new structures that were being tried out everywhere, and which culminated in a few seminal buildings of which Chartres was one of the more important. The essence of this revolution was marvellously modern. Before 1100, and indeed again after the Classical revival that followed the

Reformation, architecture was mainly concerned with walls and columns in static balance. Though domed structures were exceptional, they were on the whole built in such a solid way, and supported on such thick impenetrable walls, that they remained within the static tradition.

What these builders did was to introduce the revolutionary principle that, in planning, both forces and loads could be reduced to the abstraction of a line, or even a point. They designed the mass of the piers and buttresses out from these centres and though they appeared to concentrate these loads in the ribs and shafts inside, they actually transferred them laterally beyond the walls to the flyers outside. The solid masonry that had once defined the envelope of all earlier buildings was transformed into a thin skin or screen, often filled with glass, between which rose bundles of vertical shafts, thin flying arches and webs of ribbing that appeared to be taking all the strain.

The traditional use of blocks of stone had for thousands of years conditioned builders to think of mass in relation to size. Now these concepts of solidity and thickness were overthrown, and though the masters always concealed enough masonry behind the shafts to carry the weights, the new style was a sublime statement of this revolutionary idea. They saw that these solid and heavy realities could be expressed as one-dimensional lines having neither thickness nor weight. It was an extraordinary achievement. It made the great glass-walled cathedrals possible, and produced a dynamic architecture in which equilibrium was maintained only because one part was kept in balance against another. Remove something, and the whole could collapse. It was secure only in its entirety. They dared the elementals of wind and gravity and, in one of the most thrilling episodes in architectural history, succeeded.

It has been endlessly frustrating to admire these buildings, while knowing so little about their makers. However, the cathedrals need not be silent. Though there are no documents or legends about the great masters at Chartres, we can in fact discover an enormous amount about them. We can read the story of the cathedral's construction stone by stone. By interrogating it carefully enough we can see the artists who made it, and enter into something of their spirit. The makers of the Gothic style need not be lost. A few of them stand forth in Chartres as architects of the highest calibre with creative personalities that we can identify if we look carefully enough.

8 · CHARTRES

2

MESSINESS CAN BE A VIRTUE

WHEN YOU EXAMINE the cathedral closely, you discover to your immense surprise that the design is not a well controlled and harmonious entity, but a mess. We tend to think of a great work of art like Chartres as having been thought through to the end before it was begun. But Chartres is not like this, not at all. Our vision has been conditioned by the homogenising eye of the camera, but when we look carefully we see that there are few things at one end of the building that match those at the other. Windows and piers and buttresses change, as do hidden elements such as walls and footings, and of course all the details. The closer we look the messier it becomes: there is no other word for it.

For a start, examine the lowest courses of the outside walling. The nave has enormously heavy buttresses, some of the largest ever built. They each cover the area of a reasonably sized bedroom. Between them tall single windows light the aisles, which finish in pointed arches with small heads projecting below the drip moulds. Under the window there is a long gently sloping sill for shedding the rainwater.

There is an incomparable air of certainty about the nave. It has the simple massing of an Egyptian temple. The rhythm of buttresses and windows is an uncomplicated a–A–a–A–a. The sloping sills smoothly join one buttress to the next, while at the same time helping the solid walling of the foundation to merge vertically with the darker openings of the windows. Even the jambs seem to flow into the buttresses through the three steps that frame them. In a word, the nave is homogeneous, the masonry predominates, and the windows are a natural corollary to the buttresses.

But how different is the sanctuary! Why have we ever been deluded into thinking that it is part of the same building? It is like adding a modern glass and concrete office block to a Victorian bank: they fit

5 and 6 The lower walls of the nave on the left, and of the sanctuary on the right, which enclose the aisles. None of the details found on one side can be matched on the other.

together, for the street will absorb them both, and the tension between them merges into the rich tapestry of the city. The cathedral's reputation has, like the street, tranquillised our perceptions.

So compare carefully the sanctuary walls with those of the nave. The buttresses are thin, even meagre, and they rise with little articulation from the ground to the roof. Between them the entire wall has been eliminated, and without any frame or transition the glass stretches from buttress to buttress. The wall has disappeared, and a window has taken its place, entirely. The glass predominates, not the masonry. There is no merging underneath, either. Where the single window in the nave grows out of the sill as a tree grows from its roots, the double lancets in the choir are framed like a painting: at the sides by the buttresses and below by the strong horizontal line of the cornice. Also they are capped with a round arch instead of a pointed one, and there are no heads alongside the drip moulds.

Below the cornice there are two more horizontal mouldings which stress the plane of the wall, and separate it from the vertically oriented buttresses. Instead of the homogeneous plasticity of the nave, the sanctuary walls are an amalgam of parts. This separation of wall from glass and of both from structure feels much more modern. It is a two-dimensional elevation where the nave is three. It is an assembly of parts whose distinct functions have been emphasised by their being individually articulated.

Not only is the spirit of the design different, but so are the functions. The cornice under the window marks the edge of a walkway which passes around the eastern end of the building. There is no walkway in the nave, for the walling slopes up to the glass, both inside and out. But the walkway in the sanctuary gives access to the windows. You climb up one of the circular stairs to get on to it, and there are openings through the buttresses so that you can pass from one bay to another. The massiveness so evident in the nave has been again denied, this time by these openings which penetrate what is left of the buttresses.

Structure is essential to architecture, and along with most of my peers I have taken it for granted that a support should not be placed over a window. This is not because we cannot make a beam strong enough to carry the loads, but because it looks wrong. Loads and weights should go straight to the ground upon which everything in this world is supported. Yet, just around the corner from the sanctuary, the buttresses between the windows of the chapels were placed right over

7 The buttress-like mullions between the windows of the chapels sit over the openings into the crypt in an uneasy manner.

the centre of the crypt windows. Even the photograph (Fig. 7) makes me feel uncomfortable. In the nave, structure is an aspect of and inherent in the wall; in the sanctuary, it has been condensed into the buttresses, but here in the chapels it has been denied altogether. Three such arrangements in the one building can only be called 'messy'.

Yet underneath the chapels the curved walls round the crypt have a heaviness and a material solidity that seems to grow out of the ground itself. The simple arcs around each chapel are huge, and the deep chasms that lead to the crypt windows only enhance the stupendous solidity of the walls. Compare this part to the wall-lessness of the sanctuary. How could two such different concepts be wedded in the one building?

The traditional explanation is that the crypt walls were built by the first master in charge of the works (who also designed the nave), and that he was one of the old-timers, brilliantly if unfashionably working in the massive style of the Romanesque. He is supposed to have been succeeded by a younger man, one of the creators of the new Gothic style, who opened up the walls at the east and thinned down the buttresses. But if this is so, why are there round arches over the sanctuary windows and pointed ones in the nave? And if we can explain that away, what about the reverse situation in the crypt windows: the round arches in the nave and the pointed ones in the curved walls of the chapels? And then why are the adjoining crypt windows in the sanctuary also round like those in the nave, when the chapels are pointed? As we look closer, we surely realise that the explanation is not going to be so simple.

The 'mess' is too complex for such an easy solution. Look at the transepts and their towers. In the glass of the southern rose there are drawings of the donor, Pierre Mauclerk, the count of Dreux, and his family. Two of his children are represented, Roux born in 1217 and Yolande born in 1221. Yet we know that he had three children. His middle boy Artus is not shown. As he died in 1224, we conclude that the window should be dated some time after that, but before Pierre revolted against the queen regent, Blanche of Castille, in 1228.

The northern rose has been dated about a decade later because some of the panels have been decorated with the emblems of the royal houses of France and Castille. Blanche was regent during the minority of her son, and coming from Castille she would want to mix her family's arms with her husband's. This rose has therefore been dated

8 The south transept and porch. It is completely different from the north transept (Fig. 12) in detailing, and in the porch and buttresses.

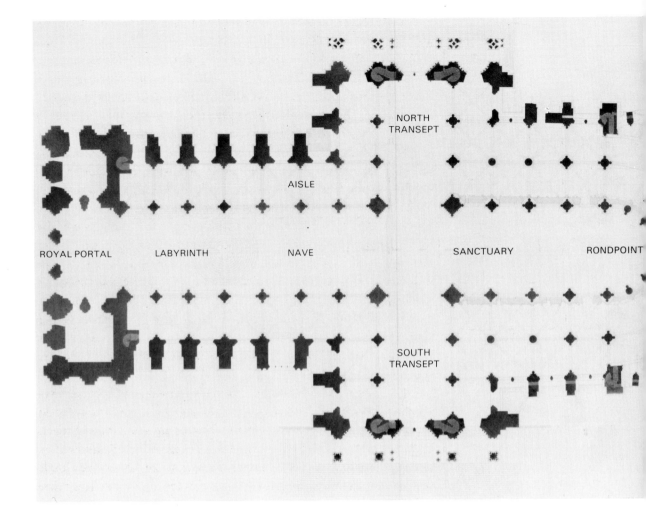

NORTH TRANSEPT

AISLE

ROYAL PORTAL LABYRINTH NAVE SANCTUARY RONDPOINT

SOUTH TRANSEPT

9 Main floor-plan of the cathedral.

from the decade of her regency, and so would be before 1236.

The stonework for the windows would naturally have been carved before the glaziers began, as the glass could not be fabricated until the shape of each opening had been accurately determined. The southern rose is therefore considered to be a little earlier than the northern. And that is the feeling we get when we look at them. Not only is the northern more crystalline and sharp-edged, but the space between it and the five lancets has also been filled with glass. Where the southern rose is just a circular opening within the masonry, the northern is the summit of a whole wall of glass. The north is closer to the incredible glazed transepts of later decades. And so for all these reasons the southern rose is thought to be the earlier one.

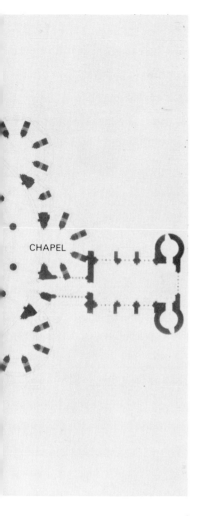

CHAPEL

Now examine the towers that flank these roses. The southern pair are encrusted bundles of shafts, starting within the openings and continuing all round the outside of the buttresses. The masonry has been hidden behind a screen of thin colonnettes that force the eye to move upwards. Compare this verticalised arrangement with the north. Not only are there no colonnettes, but the little aedicules or temples attached to the face of the buttresses arrest the eye and hold it midway up the façade. The upward movement of the south has been transformed into a centred one. The northern towers seem shorter, too, for the sill has been set higher up to suit the height of the aedicules.

There is a curious contradiction here between the towers and the windows. The colonnettes of the south and the taller elegance of the tower openings are more advanced stylistically than the squat plainer masonry of the north, yet the more progressive fully glazed window wall is placed between the older-style towers. How could this older window come to be placed within the newer tower, and vice versa? We cannot argue ourselves out of the realities of these situations. Either the building is a total confusion, in which case our feelings for what is great in art are remiss, or our concepts about architectural order are not those of the middle ages.

Let us look at another example, the one that mediaeval scholars have probably been most irritated by: the flying buttresses. As a design motif they are extraordinary, creating marvellous spaces round them. Their tall fingers of arched masonry curve overhead, rising like antlers to the windows. There is no enclosure against the sky, so the clouds and the sunlight seem to enter right into this forest of stone. It is a rare and exciting privilege to stand within these noble spaces. It takes the breath away, even in memory. The nave is massive, and seems eternal, while the choir is so light it seems to vibrate. The stolid and the elegant. What a contrast within the one building, or are we by now so habituated to differences that it makes no impact on us?

The lowest supporting arches in the nave are thick and square edged, while the choir's are thinner and the edges have been chamfered to lighten the appearance even more. The nave spokes are treated like columns, complete with bases and caps, and support sturdy round arches. They are meant to carry great loads. These thick arches and squat columns are seen to be making heavy work of the job they have to do.

The choir could not have been more differently made, even if

perversity had been the intention. The spokes are taller and thinner, and they support pointed arches. They are square, not like the round columns of the nave, and by being placed edgewise they seem to be even slenderer. Everything about them emphasises their inability to carry any loads at all, and this is enhanced by the circular opening that has been placed directly above the centre of each spoke as if it were a piece of tracery.

10 and 11 The nave flyers are robust with massive column-like spokes and thick arches. In contrast those of the choir are delicate, with a screen-like infill of pointed arches and diagonally placed webbing.

The choir is speaking a different language altogether. The function of the choir flyers is the same as the nave's, but the arches have been made to do it all. The spokes are no more than a decorative infill of no structural value, a purposeless but charming extravagance.

As with the aisle windows and the towers of the transepts, it has been argued that the nave flyers are more Romanesque in feeling, and so earlier. But the situation at this level is not clear either. Indeed it is so unclear that, despite superficial impressions, of the ten scholars who have tried over the last eighty years to determine whether the eastern end was the first part built or the last, fully half of them have decided that the more Gothic choir was built before the nave. If scholars are equally divided over the problem, it must be a complex problem indeed.

One of the complications in the choir occurs where the flyers turn the corner into the transepts. They have the same thin form as their neighbours, but the spokes have been designed like those in the nave, with caps and bases. And if you think this is deranged, what of the near-by roofs over the aisle vaults? The variety here is unbelievable.

There are low-pitched roofs made of interlocking stones forming a flat upper surface, and steep ones where the stones overlap like tiles. There are slate roofs and lead lean-tos; some have gable windows, and some rest on small cellar-like openings squeezed into the narrow space between the eaves and the walkway. Even the frames round the doorways into the rooms sheltered by these roofs are different, as are the gables over them. The profusion is mind-blowing. The silhouette from the ground is sharply serrated in some places and gently undulates in others. In some the face of the roof dominates, and in others it is hidden behind a profusion of sharp-pointed gablets.

The closer we examine the building, and the closer we come to its details, the more confusing it becomes. Of the ninety doors through which the builder gained access to every part of the building, there are few with the same plans. And of the more than fifty windows that light the staircases, there are over a dozen different types. Even in matching situations where a single design for a door or a window could have served in both places, we find that they differ. Such perversity is deeply disturbing, for where under all this confusion lies the great work of art?

Anyone walking round the cathedral knows how different the north porch is from that on the south. One explanation given for this is that they were both added after the transepts had been completed. But an examination of the stones themselves indicates that this is highly questionable. The evidence shows that the two porches were built with the transepts they abut, which were themselves built with the rest of the building. There was no more than a year or two between the setting out of the one on the north and the other on the south. If this is how things were built, how then do we explain the differences?

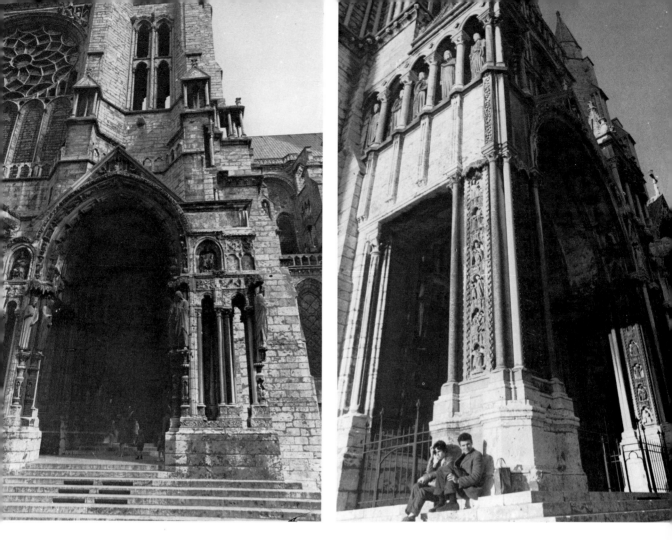

12 and 13 The south porch is light and intricately decorated. The north on the left is heavy, supported on four large shafts placed in a diamond formation surrounded by four carved piers, and its decoration is robust.

Many have noticed that in the western end of the nave the bays become smaller and smaller, until the one abutting the towers is nearly a metre narrower than the average. Yet if the nave had had six bays between the crossing and the tower instead of seven, all six could have been made the same size, and the master would not have had to cut one and a half metres into the stonework of the east face of the towers to accommodate a bay that was going to be too small anyway.

And a few careful observers have been astonished at the irregularities in the transepts. No two bays are the same size: the axes twist at almost every pier, and the end walls that support the porches are far from parallel. The confusion in the axes of the choir is even worse, though we could excuse that by saying that they had to be built upon the walls of a much older building; but this excuse will not do for the transepts, for the destroyed church did not have them. The irregularities in the transepts occur in the only part of the cathedral to have been set out from scratch.

The closer we look, the worse it becomes. Cornices change shape in the middle of a bay, and the corbels sometimes do not match from one side of the door to the other, while the lintels they support vary all over the building. Of six towers, only the northern pair were built to the same plan. One of the southern ones is an octagonal shape inside and the other is irregular, while the interior of the eastern ones are quite square. One of the eastern towers has four shafts supporting a four-part vault while the other has eight, yet there are no shafts for the ribs of any of the transept towers.

Both in the details and in the general concept, the building is far from being a single piece, with the one exception of the interior elevation. It is splendid, and has been hailed as one of the most influential designs in the middle ages, forming a prototype from which many later buildings were derived. From one end to the other, except in small variations, the interior is uniform.

This may not sound like a very significant boast, for shouldn't all great buildings have homogeneous interiors? But do they? In Notre-Dame in Paris, the shape of the piers changes a number of times down the length of the building, as do the transept walls and the windows of the clerestory. The important church at Laon with its elegant towers is similar, while in smaller buildings like the abbey churches at Orbais and Essomes, south-west of Reims, and in parish churches all over the place, the interiors change radically from one section to the next. Uniformity is the exception rather than the rule, inside as well as out.

Beyond the sight of the clergy officiating at the mass, and of the tourists being told the stories of the windows, the building is an endless profusion of differences. Faced with this, is it any wonder that historians have attempted to explain the confusion as coming from different periods of construction? At Noyon, where over eighty years separated one part of the building from another, or at Soissons where the southern transept was begun in 1173, the choir over twenty years later and the northern transept a century later on, we can see the breaks between the campaigns in the radical changes in style between the work of one epoch and the next. But Chartres is substantially the work of one generation. The upper parts are of course some decades later than the lower, but on any one level there cannot be many years between one arm and the next. We know that the building must have been entirely set out within a few years of the fire of 1194, and that within three decades both ends had been completed to the vaults. So the confusion and messiness of Chartres cannot be explained as simply as other buildings, as the result of different eras of construction.

The boundaries between the changes are not so simply organised that they point to clean breaks between one large campaign and another. They are too mixed up, and there are too many of them. Ideas that could at one level be associated with one master keep on turning up in areas that other things indicate we should be attributing to another. It is as though the workshop had a large box, full of templets of all shapes and sizes collected from all over France, and that each week or so the master rummaged among them to choose the one that suited his fancy on that particular day. The distribution of outlines and alterations is random enough to give this crazy impression.

The confusion in the building is reflected in the confusion among historians, who cannot agree on the overall chronology, let alone the parts. In the nineteenth century it was assumed that the cathedrals were built bay by bay, in sections from the pier to the vaults. As a result, most people have presumed that the western and eastern ends of the building must have come from separate campaigns, and without being precise, many seem to have concluded that therefore one end in its entirety must have been the product of a different campaign to the other. This has led them to concentrate on trying to determine which was the first, and in this they have been led astray. Perhaps it came from looking at the public parts of the cathedral, those seen by the outside observer, rather than from examining the private parts as they would have been seen by the builder. When the stones are examined, piece by piece, from the experienced standpoint of a builder or an architect, the answers can be found.

Truly, the stones themselves do speak. The staircases that the masons used for access, the rooms under the towers, the walkways around the outside and in particular the attic rooms behind the triforium passage are the builder's territory. It is here, in these unlit and seldom visited spaces, that the answers are to be found. And it is as unexpected as it is clear, once understood.

The arguments about chronology in the end turned out to be irrelevant, for there was no break between the eastern and western ends. The choir and the nave had been built together, though one end was always a little ahead of the other. The architectural evidence shows that the entire building was constructed in layers from the ground up, without any vertical breaks at all, and that work on it was continued without interruption from the time of the fire to the completion of the last vaults over the northern rose.

Now that we recognise the chaotic nature of the building, how can we explain the extraordinary impact it has on people? We feel that Chartres is one of the greatest works of art created by man; but if it is, what part does unity play in great art? And if we cannot attribute the confusion in the design to different eras of building work, how can we explain the mess? In periods of transition like this time, at the turn of the thirteenth century, in which the style we call Romanesque was being transformed into the revolutionary forms of Gothic, we cannot date by style. When many ideas are being bandied about, no one thing is more progressive than another. Only time and the choices made by their successors decide that one. When there may be only a dozen years between parts of the work, changes in form can seldom indicate the date. It would be like trying to fix, seven hundred years from now, the relative chronology of Picasso's 'Guernica' from his late classical drawings and his Blue period, when we do not know whether they were by one artist or many, or have any clues to the identity of the painter. We can only become as receptive as possible, cool down our preconceptions, and let the building tell its own tale. It will, given the chance.

3
THE CONTRACTORS

THERE ARE A NUMBER of ill-lit rooms behind the triforium arcade. They are like attics, for the roof slopes down to within a few feet of the floor. The walls separating one bay from another are quite thick, and the openings through them have corbels at the top which support the lintel. Corbels are one of the features to be found all over the cathedral. There is hardly an opening that is not crowned with them, and you can easily see many of them from the ground. That at the top of Fig. 15 is one of eight on the south side of the nave, and though there are slight

14 This opening through the cross wall of the attic space at triforium level joins the rooms behind the triforium arcade. The arcade itself lies on the other side of the wall on the left, and can be seen in Fig. 3.

variations between them, they all belong to the same family.

On the other side of the nave is another group of corbels. They have none of the individuality to be found in the south. Within a millimetre or two they all have the same shape, which is no mean achievement in this hard and brittle limestone. I have held sheets of cardboard against the faces of the corbels and traced their shapes directly. Even in the curves, the variation from one to the other is minuscule.

These northern ones are cut from larger stones than the southern, and the joints between them are smaller. The chiselling is quite exquisite, even on stones that are tucked out of sight. They come from another part of the quarry, for the stone is more even in texture with few if any of the fissures that disfigure the southern walling.

On returning to the south I noticed that the stonework lying above the corbels was decidedly closer to that from which the northern corbels themselves had been made, and on looking at the north again I saw that the lower stonework in the lower part of the walls was rougher, and more like the other side. There seem to have been two crews of workmen, one taking stones from a poorer part of the quarry and with only average standards of workmanship, and another with higher standards in all things, in finishing, cutting, in the selection of the stone itself and in placement. It is enough to look at the mortar joints between their stones to see that their standards were immeasurably superior to those of the rougher crew.

I then noticed there was evidence for a third crew sitting above the excellent one. This work was pretty ragged, with long thin stones often only roughly axed and with joints that were sometimes so crude that they had to be packed out with small stones. The area of work done by this crew was clearly defined, for every second stone had a mark carved on it.

These are called mason's marks—the individual signatures of the cutters. Some are quite ordinary, like crosses or circles, or letters such as A and T. But some are magnificent, forming fine abstract designs, or even objects like water-jars and pentagons. The ones used in Chartres are not outstanding, but I have seen a wolf at Tours, and in Southwell a hooded man and a superb fish, and a fine set of variations on the letter A at Durham. We do not know as much about these marks as we would like to, but they often indicated that the men at the quarry were paid by the piece rather than by the day. The mason marked each stone as it left his banker, so they could be tallied at the end of the day. This

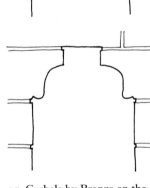

15 Corbels by Bronze on the south side of the nave, and by Scarlet on the north.

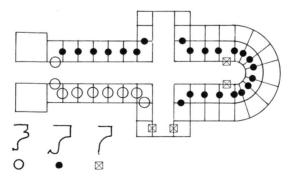

16 Olive's mason's marks and his corbel, and below a sampling of marks in other buildings.

means that the more they cut the more they were paid, and might explain the poorer quality of this part of the walling.

The stones with the mason's marks lie above those of the other two crews. There is no mingling. The junctions between the work of one crew and the next are quite distinct. In the choir, one of these marks appears on the same stone as a corbel. It is another type altogether, and quite unlike the previous two.

It was then that I realised that I was staring at the proof that the nave and the choir had been built at the same time, and not in two separate campaigns. The controversies of the previous eighty years — between those who thought that the choir had been built before the nave, and their opponents — was at one stroke a thing of the past. The proof was simple, yet totally convincing.

First, the corbels cut by the second crew, the big ones made with such exquisite workmanship, were to be found not only on the north side of the nave, but over all the openings of the choir as well. And the corbels on the southern side of the nave carved by the crew of average workmanship were to be found at both ends of the building, as were the stones covered with mason's marks. Finally these mason's marks are

17 The distribution of corbels within the triforium attic rooms by Bronze, Scarlet and Olive.

almost the only ones to be found anywhere in the thirteenth-century part of the building, and the only ones to be found in quantity. The distribution of the corbels around the triforium, as can be seen in Fig. 17, bear out this argument. Particularly notice the presence of one of the southern nave corbels on the north side, and those with the mason's marks on both sides of the southern transept.

It would be rather coincidental to find three crews appearing in the same order on both sides of the building, and finishing much the same quantity of work at each end, were the nave and choir not being built at the same time. These three clearly and uniquely discernible layers of work succeeding one another in the same order at both ends show that the two arms of the cathedral were built at the same time. However, the actual arrangement of the corbels and stone types shows that the western extremity was more advanced than the east, and the southern side generally a little ahead of the north.

The building was therefore not constructed in bays, nor one arm at a time, but in layers. Each layer was the work of a separate building contractor, and the corbel seems to have been his especial mark. In one sense it was his signature. In the bulk of the thirteenth-century part of the cathedral, excluding only the last campaigns on the gables that stretched into the second half of the century, there are only nine corbels and, as I came to realise, nine contractors.

I decided to name these corbels, and the builders they represented, for when something is named it begins to acquire a life of its own, a reality. I felt I was going to need all the co-operation I could get if these contractors were to become alive. We have no documented names in Chartres, and even in other buildings where a few names do occur, we can only seldom be sure they refer to the contractor. Clerical Latin is frustratingly imprecise about building matters. The man variously referred to as the 'master of the works' or 'of the fabric' could have been the builder, but he could just as well have been the clerk of works appointed by the clergy to keep his eye on the job, or the master mason or architect himself, or even the general maintenance man.

To avoid these problems altogether, I sought other names for them. Ones like 'the master of the Gallic foot' or 'of the fallen arch' or 'the missing voussoir' obviously would not do, and to christen them 'Bert' or 'Fred' would create confusion later if we did find names to attach to these crews. I finally chose colours, partly because I once dreamt of publishing a history of the cathedral in colour rather than in the black-

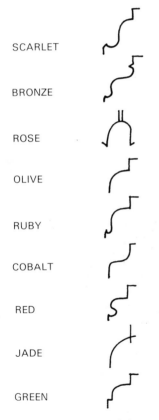

SCARLET

BRONZE

ROSE

OLIVE

RUBY

COBALT

RED

JADE

GREEN

18 The contractors, their names, and the symbols I use for them, which are derived from their corbels.

and-white that the necessities of inflation and recession force upon us.

The first crew with the average stonework I christened Bronze, the second whose standards were so high Scarlet, and the third with the mason's marks Olive. The names of the other six are set out in Fig. 18 with their corbels.

Gradually I learnt more and more about these men, though the mistakes and false trails were innumerable, and often hopelessly disheartening. I began by isolating all the joints I could find that would show where one crew was replaced by another. Some were easy, like the cornice under the triforium walkway shown in Fig. 20. The one on the right projects more than the left, and the section through each is quite different. Some time later, after I had analysed all the cornices in the building, I came to the conclusion that the right-hand ones were by Bronze and the left were by Olive. They had been laid while these crews were working on the walls of the triforium attic.

There is also a difference in the way the crockets have been arranged on the stones. Bronze on the right cut each stone to suit the size of the crocket, as there is only one on each block, while Olive on the left did the reverse. There may be one, or two, or even three per stone. He arranged his crockets to suit the lengths of the blocks as they came out of the quarry. In itself this may not seem an important observation, but taken with many others it has helped me to understand something about the men in charge of the crews.

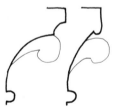

19 and 20 On the right in the photo is the cornice over the eastern window out of the southern transept, just under the triforium walkway. The shape of the stone obviously changes in mid-span, shown above. Bronze's is on the left and Olive's on the right.

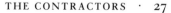

Bronze is not only more punctilious than Olive, as we have already seen in the quality of the stones that each had cut for the triforium, but he is more integrative. The crockets Bronze used affected the size of the block cut. His decoration is not an incidental part of the building, but essential. These attitudes can be found in other work by the same masters. Bronze always varied the size of the corbels over his doors to suit the height of the openings, while Olive used the same-sized corbel no matter how big the door. Olive just added items to the building, be they crockets or corbels, while Bronze integrated them so that they fused. We can certainly say that the sort of person who led one crew could not have led the other.

Not many of the ten thousand or so joints I isolated in the building were as obvious as this one in the cornice, but once I learnt what to look for, I found them. Each time the key was to search for the changes in the mouldings. For mouldings were cut by the stonemason to shapes marked on a wooden board, called a templet. The form of the templet was made personally by the master, and would therefore be a major indication of his identity. I found myself measuring more and more. The sloping upper face of a drip mould would change from 165 mm to 190 mm; the height of the triforium arcade columns was reduced 50 mm between the nave and the choir; the jambs around doors, the diameter of shafts, the splays on the tops of plinths all changed and added to my growing collection of different templets.

I had to distinguish between those changes that were the choice of the stonemason and those that came from the master himself. Those that were scattered randomly would be the work of the individual, like the arrangement of leaves on capitals and bosses. But where one shape was continued unchanged over a number of contiguous stones, I felt I was looking at a form that came from the master. Where one group stopped and another began, I felt I might have found a joint, and would start looking for additional evidence that might corroborate it.

For example, under the columns of the triforium arcade there is a continuous plinth that forms a dwarf wall alongside the passage. The plinth is reduced at the top by two splays to suit the bases of the columns that sit on it. In the western bays of the nave the outside splay is steeper than the inside one, and the joints between the stones occur under the columns. Then near the crossing the splays change. They are cut to the same slope on each side, and the top face is smaller, at 395 mm instead of 405 mm. The joints are still under the columns, but

3 EQUAL DIVISIONS

21 Section through the triforium passage showing unequal slopes on top of the plinth.

now the stones have been tied together with iron cramps set into the top face. A few bays further on, the splays and the dimensions change again, the iron cramps disappear and the joints are no longer placed under the columns, but are merely the accidental result of the length of the stones as they come out of the quarry. These ones, predictably, turned out to be Olive's.

Confirmation of this analysis came when I found that the width of most of the column bases sitting on the first set of plinths was smaller than the top, with a 5 mm gap on either side. These smaller bases would have exactly suited the width of the second set of plinths, suggesting that the same templet had cut both. These correlations could then be extended into the bases and plinths of the third group, and so on.

Such a painstaking analysis helped me to visualise, stone by stone, the order in which everything had been cut and placed. After the first plinths had been laid there was a pause in the construction, and when the next master arrived he had a new templet cut so that the plinths could be continued to the east. Either he did not notice that the slopes differed from the earlier ones, or he thought that unequal slopes were crazy. The 405 mm upper face was too wide for the bases he wished to put under the shafts, so he reduced the width of his plinths. He did not increase the size of the bases that were to sit over the earlier larger plinths. On the contrary, he cut them to suit the new templet, and accepted the gap left on either side as a small price to pay for getting them right. In other areas we have examples of bases being wider than the plinth, where presumably the master saw no incongruity in cutting them to the size he preferred, even though it meant that they had to overhang the edge. These examples convinced me that the master was prepared to order his men to carry out the work his way, even if there were small misfits where his stones met his predecessor's.

This sequence was handsomely confirmed when I came to analyse the carving on the caps and to compare those in the triforium with other parts of the building and in the choir buttresses. The plans of the buttresses were changed from a Greek cross to an octagon between Bronze's work and Scarlet's, and the square pilasters under the southern towers were changed into angled ones between Scarlet's and Olive's campaigns. Not all of these other pieces of evidence involved complete changes to the mouldings, but usually only the particulars of their shape. If a cornice had been started, it would not suddenly be

22 Section through the cathedral showing the joint between Scarlet's campaign and Olive's in 1209.

changed into a string course or omitted altogether, but the outline would be altered.

On the other hand, some of the forms used may have been standardised as hallmarks of the job. The imposts over the capitals are much the same shape throughout the building, and look a little like the Bronze corbel in outline. The imposts in other churches would also follow a pattern, often quite different from the one used here, in spite of the fact that the same crews worked on all the buildings. The ones at Brie-Compte-Robert, east of Paris, are Cobalt's, at Lagny they may be Olive's, while those at Chartres were begun by Bronze. There seems to have been an understanding that a certain uniformity would be maintained throughout the job by continuing to use the same format for some mouldings, once it had been established. Yet each master continued to vary the templet slightly as his interpretation of the job standard, so even in repeated mouldings we can still follow the breaks between the campaigns.

As you can see, the processes of joint-hunting, of measurement and of reconstructing the building sequence went hand in hand. The plinths showed me that in any one course of the building I should expect to find the work of half a dozen contractors. This was because one end of the cathedral was always a metre or so higher than the other, and when the first plinths were being laid in the south-west corner of the nave some of the eastern chapels were still being vaulted, and by the time they were ready for the plinths all the nave triforium columns had been set up and the passage was about to be roofed over.

To visualise this, examine the section through the building drawn by Lassus and Durand over a hundred years ago (Fig. 22). On it I have drawn the joint between Scarlet's campaign and Olive's.

There were technical aspects of the building that helped me to locate joints, too, though many would not have been noticed by the layman. For example there are three methods for attaching the voussoirs of the arch, be it round or pointed, to the wall. Bronze and Olive both used the first, Scarlet and Ruby the second and Cobalt the third. There is a philosophy behind each one, as there is in all building decisions (Fig. 23).

The bottom stone in the second example is like an anchor that locks the arch into the wall and helps to transfer the side thrusts into the masonry that can absorb them. In the first there is no attempt to express visually the direction of these forces. The arch is seen as a self-contained unit within the wall, while in the third the arch seems to grow out of the bottom stone, as a plant grows out of the ground. We shall see later that Cobalt may have visualised structural forces in this verdant manner, acting in both directions, up and down, while Bronze has the audacity to think that he could shunt his thrusts to and fro as he thought best.

If these ideas seem peculiar, remember that we are examining a building designed eight centuries ago, when there were no mathematical tools for analysing structure, either statically or dynamically, and that model testing was unheard of. Yet, without these tools, they attempted to analyse and contain the forces acting within some of the tallest structures ever built. Roofs and stone vaults and tall walls are all

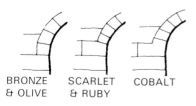

BRONZE & OLIVE   SCARLET & RUBY   COBALT

23 Three ways of handling the arch springing.

subject to impressive wind loads, which must be carried to the ground. Combined with settlement and weak mortar, everything seems to have conspired to push these buildings over, and answers had to be devised somehow, no matter how tenuous the evidence on which the reasoning might be based.

Foundations were a matter of guesswork, based certainly on experience but without any way of being verified, and once built they were seldom checked when the height of the building was increased or when towers were added over walls or footings, even though they had not always been designed for them. Under these conditions the structural concepts they developed were inevitably somewhat weird. The fact that their works continue to stand is a memorial to their practical rather than to their theoretical skills.

Yet every builder has to have some theoretical rules to help him to solve problems. They are the mnemonics of the industry, being the only way that experience can be memorised and taught. In the end, the final proof of an idea lay in the building. If it stood up, an idea worked; if it collapsed, then one of the rules had failed. Collapses were far from uncommon: towers, walls, and indeed entire buildings fell down from time to time. The masters must have come from far and wide to examine the débris for hints of what might have gone wrong. How else could they have learnt? As far as we know, nothing at Chartres ever actually fell down, though the centering under the vaults at the top of the southern choir tower shifted while the ribs were being laid. The piers were pushed outwards, and it would not have taken much more for them to have toppled altogether. As they supported the flyers to the choir, much of the sanctuary—finished only four years before—may have collapsed too. A close call. The lean can still be seen in Fig. 33.

Two hundred years before Chartres, when the first stone churches were being built in the north of Europe after a hiatus that was almost as long, the builders had simple rules to help them to work out their sizes. For example, a square would be drawn inside the walls of the nave and, to calculate the outside, a circle would be set around the square, as in the Saxon church of Bradford-on-Avon. A simple rule for small buildings, but one which would have made the walls too thick if the span had been increased. As buttresses were added to the outside of the wall, was this $\sqrt{2}$ ratio to be taken to the outside of the buttress, or should the builders rethink the problem, and evolve another one? As shafts were added to the inside, was the interior to be measured to the

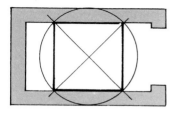

24 Plan of the nave of Bradford-on-Avon showing how the wall thickness relates to the interior as $\sqrt{2}:1$.

wall face, or to the centre of the shaft which 'represented' the loads from the roof, or to some axis within the wall? And when aisles were added, the problems became even more complex.

The number of rules had to be increased as architecture developed in complexity. Not having testing techniques for assessing the validity of each one, the builders resorted to reason. But reason in the absence of fact is just another name for art. Gradually over many generations the masters evolved an intellectually satisfying methodology for handling these rules. It was at heart an aesthetic one in which different and often mathematically irreconcilable rules were combined and, by various stratagems, brought into a synthesis.

This way to approach a problem is very mediaeval. One of the techniques of scholastic dialectics was to pose an opinion, to set it against a contrary opinion and out of the ensuing discussion to evolve a synthesis. The posing of opposites and their reconciliation was a cultural trait. They believed that as God had created the world, every part of it would reflect his Essence. This was extended to buildings in which every detail and element had to reflect the whole, just as the whole in the numbers and forms used in the design was to express God himself. This was done through geometry, which was applied to every part, no matter how small. No moulding or window or plinth was arranged without it. Geometry totally pervaded the building.

But building techniques did not evolve out of theory alone. Construction is a practical affair. In every organisation where one man relies on others to carry out his ideas, there must be clear and simple ways to pass them on. To be able to delegate work to others, there must be some way to communicate them unambiguously. For thousands of years architects have issued instructions to masons and carpenters, and these proven techniques were inherited by the contractors of the middle ages. The techniques were essentially geometric. Their geometry was not theoretical, like Euclid's theorems, but practical. Their tools were the compass, straight-edge and ruler, angles, proportional dividers and string. Do not undervalue the string, for without it no building can be laid out, even today.

In working with these tools they were naturally drawing circles, squares and triangles. Doodle with them yourself and you will effortlessly come up with geometric forms. The tools and the methods go together. Only through geometry could the master be certain that the templet being cut for a moulding would be the same as the one he had used last time, and that the outline of one stone would therefore exactly match its neighbour. It made for repeatability, and therefore for precision.

An inestimably useful tool, it is no wonder that over the centuries geometry acquired a certain mystery. It was the technique that made the cathedrals possible. It allowed one man to control and direct the work of hundreds successfully towards one common goal. Also, through the analogies that numbers and shapes have always had to abstract ideas, it became the method for translating important theological concepts into stone. Without geometry great and laborious building works are inconceivable.

Early in the middle ages, geometry consisted mainly of simple numerical ratios, such as 5:8, called harmonics, and easy geometric figures such as squares and triangles. By the time Chartres was being built, these techniques had become more complex, spurred on by the growing intricacy of the buildings themselves and by the masons' determination to resolve the opposing ideas that were developing within the different geometries they were using, no matter how difficult this might be.

I will give examples of this later on, but as I investigated the masters' ways of handling geometry, I found that each had his own rules. Almost none was universally accepted. Even at the end of the middle ages Gil de Hotendon was sent from Seville to the north to find the correct rules for building buttresses, and returned complaining that no two authorities could give him the same answers.

In time I was able to identify the master of a door or a window, or even of a whole room, from the geometry and the foot unit used in it. For example, take this window by the contractor Rose. It is one of more than fifty narrow windows that give light on to the stairs. This one looks out of the south-west stair into the space between the lintels of the south porch.

In Fig. 26 you can see that the stairs are set behind one of the projections between the doorways. A recess separates the wide projection on the left from the narrow one with the single column on the right. Rose began the geometry from the corner of this recess. He extended the side of the pilaster inwards from V until it met the curve of the stairwell at A. From A he drew a line to the outside forming a 45° angle as shown.

He then placed his compass-point on A and marked two arcs along

25 Two of the windows
looking out of the stairs in the
southern porch. The upper one
that will be considered next is
by Scarlet, and the lower is by
Bronze.

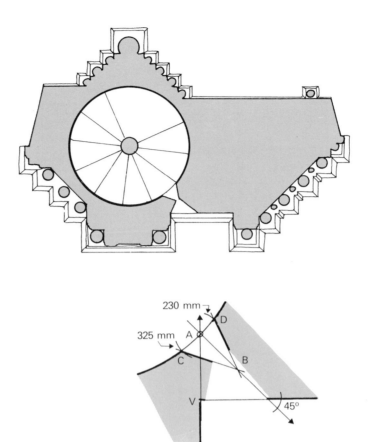

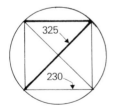

26 The south-west stairs
between the left door and the
central door. The window
looks into the porch.

27 The square and its diagonal
produced the two dimensions
used in the window.

the wall of the stairwell. One measured 325 mm and the other
230 mm, marked C and D. Lines were then drawn joining them to B,
the centre of the 45° line. The inside of the window was now fixed,
reflecting the edge of the pilaster and these two measurements.

These two lengths are related to one another through the square. If
the square has each side measuring 230 mm, then the diagonal will be
325 mm. This was a favourite mediaeval technique for producing a
series of lengths related to one another, and may be what they meant
when they referred to 'true measure'.

Having formed the inside, return to the corner of the pilaster and
the recess V. Stretch a string-line between V and the centre of the stair
newell. Bisect the wall thickness along this line at W, and draw the line
at right angles to this that will cut the inside splays at X and Y. Along
the outside wall mark the distance of 650 mm, or twice the 325 mm
used inside, and join Y to it. On the other side I would like to think that

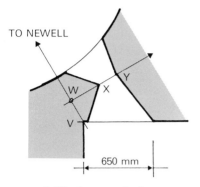

TO NEWELL

W X Y V

650 mm

28 The last stage in the geometry of this window.

Rose would have joined X to V, but as the side of the lintel also passed through V, rather than cutting the edge of the window jamb to a sharp point, he moved it in a whisker. A practical move that allowed him to cut a difficult stone.

Part of the window was evolved from the conditions round about, but two steps have been taken by using a length. 325 mm is one of the better-known foot units from the north of France and is sometimes called the *pied-du-roi*. I found as I penetrated deeper and deeper into the geometry at Chartres that a number of foot units turned up which I had not heard of before. I felt I had to know when a measure might be a foot, and when not. Was there such a thing as The Foot, or was there an infinite possible range? I found, at least for pre-mediaeval times, that there was a limited number, and that most of them went back thousands of years into antiquity and disappeared into the mists of time. The return of civilised learning did not bring with it the same regard for standard measurement. The ancient units were still to be found, but with a greater range that grew with time until by the end of the seventeenth century the confusion was huge enough to daunt the hardiest reformer.

The *pied-du-roi* was supposed to have been a gift to Charlemagne from Haroun-al-Rascid about AD 789, but it had been used in France and England long before that. It was one of the measures adopted by the Moslems during the Conquest, but even then it was old. It has been found in the Minoan civilisation of Crete, and in ancient Egypt, and may have originated on the Persian plateau some five thousand years ago. Its value has not changed by more than a couple of millimetres over the centuries.

So here in this window Rose has unambiguously exposed his foot unit. Each master had his own measure, and carried it with him engraved on an iron square, for he used it to precisely the same value each time he returned to the job. It was one of the talismans of the team, and began every independent operation. Beyond it the geometry will proliferate, through methods and ideas that the master may have learnt, or which appealed to him. But the foot he inherited with his gloves and tools from the previous master, for I have found the same foot being used by one contractor over a period of a century and a half. It is more than the mark of the man, it is the unit of the organisation.

To understand Rose a little more we can examine the feeling behind his geometry. The forms and principles that guided him tell us something about him as an artist. See how he placed the centre of the window along the bisector of the wall, which expresses not just its depth at W, but its changing thickness as stair and facade move away from one another. Symmetrically placed splays would have been inert, where this is dynamic. If he had formed the inside splays equally on either side of AB, we would have missed that lopsidedness that seems to swing the window from stair to porch. It would have expressed the stair only. By using two lengths from his 'true measure', he formed an eccentric and therefore living form.

The interior of the window is related to the facade wall. The centre is related to the wall thickness, while the outside, which is derived from the others, relates to both. Thus Rose designed the sides you can see from the street as the last step, not wanting to form such a public part too obviously. His geometry is coherent and his basic forms are simple, yet the order of his steps are so devious that the spectator sees the harmony without ever being aware of the method.

The window immediately under this looks, at first glance, somewhat similar. The staircase has the same relationship to the recess, and there is really no reason why they should differ. But when you place the plan of one over the other you see the differences clearly (Fig. 29).

Where Rose's is an open swinging form, this one is tightly closed. Where the former grew out of an interior arrangement only subtly expressed on the outside, the lower one, as you can readily see, was formed from two 45° triangles, and the outside has been resolutely aligned to the side of the buttress projection. It is the work of Scarlet.

Scarlet used two foot measures. One was the Roman of 295 mm, which is often to be found in mediaeval buildings. It survived the break-up of the Roman Empire in continental Europe, although it almost entirely disappeared in England. However, Roman is not really the correct name for it, as it has been found in the middle east in monuments and rods from almost two thousand years before the seven hills grew into a city. Scarlet's second foot was six-fifths of the Roman, and has been called the Pes Manualis, the foot-and-hand. Many masters used more than one foot at a time. There were big advantages to be gained from this, as different parts of a door or a column could be determined from each, and would automatically impart to the whole the ratio between them. In this window Scarlet used the second. He opened his compass to one-and-a-half Pes Manualis and, placing the

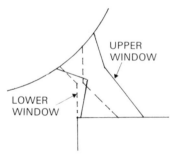

29 The lower window drawn in broken lines looks quite unlike the one immediately above it.

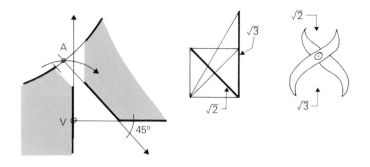

30 First stage in setting out the lower window, and on the right a pair of proportional dividers. The geometry of the $\sqrt{2}:\sqrt{3}$ ratio is shown in the middle.

point at V, drew an arc to where it cut the wall of the stairwell at A. In the second step he drew the line from A to the outside at 45°.

He next divided the space between A and the 45° line into two, in the proportion of $\sqrt{2}:\sqrt{3}$. The same proportion occurs in every one of his windows and in many mouldings, so it would have been a standard. It looks fearsome mathematically, but is in fact a surprisingly easy ratio to construct, using just a square and an equilateral triangle. If he had to construct this ratio anew each time it would have been a pretty tedious business, but one of the commonest tools used by the masters was the proportional dividers. As one pair of legs is longer than the other, the spaces between its points will always maintain the same relationship, no matter what size the opening. A pair divided into the proportion of $\sqrt{2}:\sqrt{3}$ merely had to be set on to the templet for the required division to be made in seconds without any further elaboration.

From where the inner of these 45° lines met VA at X, he drew a line parallel to the wall, and where that met the next 45° line at Y he drew another in towards the stairwell parallel to VA. These four lines formed the window, all in six steps. What could be simpler?

There are four of these windows looking out of the four staircases into the north and south porches. No two are exactly the same. This is because the relationship between the stair and the recess is slightly different in each case.

The windows have been set out anew each time, so that they precisely reflect the unique conditions around them. The geometric process was the same, yet no common templet was made that would do them all. The master designed each one as if it was for the first time. We would not do that today. We would standardise where Scarlet would not. He believed that each part of the building should precisely reflect the situation around it. No standardised unit could do this. Close as each might be to the ideal, no common shape was acceptable,

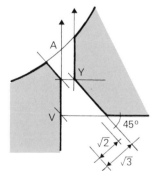

31 The second stage of the lower window.

for only perfect correspondence would do. Be it finicky or super-stitious, the cathedral is riddled with other examples. It seems to reflect a desire for unity far more intensive than anything we know today.

Unlike Rose, Scarlet did not hide his geometry. Plain 45° triangles form both sets of splays. The thickness of the wall determined the location of the inside splays, while the dividers determined the width of the slot. Everything is orderly and clear, and oriented to the outside so that the spectator can immediately relate to the thickness of the wall and to the position of the stairs. Compared with Rose's, this window is direct, straightforward and lucid.

See how simple the tools are. There is string, a rule, a square or right angle, compass and proportional dividers. What more? Everything can be constructed from them alone. And this will be so with all the geometry found in the cathedral. The masters seldom used really complex figures, so the setting out and the cutting of the templets could be kept as simple as possible. Each had his own foot measure. He carried it with him from place to place, and maintained its accuracy to the millimetre. It was probably engraved in the metal rule or square, along with its subdivisions. The palm or third of the foot was common, as was the one-and-a-half foot or cubit. Below that there were either inches or digits that divided the foot into twelfths or sixteenths.

There were no universal foot units in the middle ages, at least not in standards as we know them. There was no one unit for each country, or even for each region. There were hundreds. Each town had its own, often maintained in a metal replica set up in some public place so that strangers could equate the foot of their own region with the local one. In Vienna the two foot units were attached to the wall of the cathedral doorway, and in Dunkeld the local Ell is still fixed to the wall of one of the houses which overlooks the market.

There were usually many foot units in every town. There was a unit for the cloth-makers, and another for the customs officer and for the timber merchant. Standards encompassing more than a single trade or place were non-existent. Every merchant on coming into a market town had to discount his own measure, and his money too, against the locally-used units. He was constantly adapting one to the other, and so was daily using ratios in trade, just as the masters were in building. To think in ratios was an essential aspect of mediaeval life.

Scarlet, the first master of the cathedral, used the ancient Roman foot of 295 mm, which must have been used continuously through the

Dark Ages, for his is identical to the millimetre with the one used in Imperial times. Bronze used one of the oldest and most widespread units, known from India to Ireland, and still accepted today as one-third of the metre, known as the Teuton foot. Only one of the Chartres masters, Rose, used the Royal foot of 325 mm, while Ruby employed the English foot. Had Ruby come from one of the Norman areas? Had Rose been trained in the king's works? Had Scarlet or an earlier leader of this team been to Rome? Some day we may know, though it will not be easy. The foot outlasted the master. It was the unit of the crew, and was passed from one generation to the next. There are wills in which the master left his foot to his successor, specifically mentioning it as a precious object. Maybe the foot was to the master what the sceptre was to the ruler himself, the talisman of his authority. I fear that the origin of the units used by each crew may, like the origin of the units themselves in ancient times, be for ever lost in the earliest and unrecorded years of mediaeval history.

To all this accumulating information about geometry and foot units I added what I knew about their details, such as cornices and doors and windows, and also their ways of working stone and their technical ideas, so that slowly but surely a dossier was created. It was a long, difficult and often painful task. But as I became more familiar with the contractors, I could follow their work layer by layer across the entire building. To understand it properly and to ensure that I was not kidding myself I drew a series of bird's-eye views called axonometrics. There was one for each campaign, and they showed me what the new master would see when he arrived on the site. They helped me to understand the decisions he made, the changes and the mistakes. Though they were tedious to draw and horribly time-consuming, they taught me how they built the cathedrals.

Again and again the joints occurred at the same positions, at the sill line, the arcade springing, below window arches, cornices, vault ribs and cells, and so on. These are the places where the builder had to pause during the construction, and he was more likely to leave during a pause than anywhere else. When an arch is erected, a wooden formwork or centering has to be built first, and then the voussoirs are placed over that, and the mortar allowed to set before the centering is removed or, as we say, struck.

This could take up to six months, as the mortar was not made from cement, as ours is, but from lime, and stayed green for a long time.

32 Axonometric of the cathedral from the south-east. This is how it would have appeared at the end of Ruby's campaign, which was the thirteenth. The date will be 1206. You can see how the work is higher at the west than at the east and how the difficult and complex work around the aisle vaults is being carried out some time after those in the nave where they are just beginning to build the walls of the triforium attics.

Some thirteenth-century mortar above the vaults at Soissons was found not fully set after it was damaged in the 1914 war, and that was after seven centuries. Yet without weak mortar, paradoxical as it may seem, many of these mediaeval buildings would have collapsed years ago. They have all settled and moved over the years, and these mortars have cracked easily, and then proceeded to re-set in the new position. Alive and adaptable, the buildings would adjust themselves to the stresses placed on them to a surprising degree, so that circumstances that would have destroyed a stronger building would merely have bent a mediaeval one.

Thus the ribs and arches had to be left on their centering until the mortar had at least begun to set, and this could have taken many months. In a large building like Chartres there would always have been something else for the men to do, so they would not have built themselves out of a job. This is why there was no reason for them to remove the tilt in the work, for as you can see in the axonometric, walling and filling could be continued at one end while vaults were being placed in the middle and formwork built at the other. In smaller buildings, like the charming royal chapel of Sainte Chapelle in Paris, and where presumably there was more than adequate finance, there were changes in the contractors at each of these necessary junctions. The first master left after setting up the vault ribs and arches, the second only a few metres later having built the cells over them, but the third not only filled over this for the next floor level but continued the whole of the upper chapel up to the next necessary pause at the level of the high vaults 20 metres up.

In Chartres, these horizontal junctions are most clearly observed inside the six service stairs that rise from the floor to the roof. Each one has more than 220 treads, and they spiral inexorably to the top of the building. I found these stairs were the most valuable part of the cathedral, for in them each master could be entirely himself. The client did not rule him here, so he could design his doors and windows exactly as he pleased.

We are extremely fortunate to have so many stairs at Chartres. Few other buildings are so well endowed. In some there are none at all in areas where we need them. Yet it was only within the stairs that the large areas of plain walling could be profitably analysed, and it was only here that the triforium and other horizontal layers could be tied together, and the confusion turned to order.

The mess in fact was the stimulant, showing up the phases of the construction and leading me deeper and deeper into the history of the cathedral. As the pieces in the puzzle fitted together, and the patterns became clearer in the axonometrics, the differences between the contractors and their campaigns established themselves with some certainty.

Once we scale down our observations, and reduce our field of vision to the single stone instead of looking at whole bays or elements, the building becomes a much more orderly place. Instead of asking the big questions such as which end was first, we can let the small preponderate, and ask who laid this course, or why was that detail changed. In this way the enormous problems posed in the previous chapter can be brought down to a manageable size.

The way the building grew, and the reasons for the great differences between the nave and the sanctuary, can now be cleared up. Examine the horizontal moulding in the sanctuary placed half-way between the ground and the windows. It butts into the sides of the buttresses without continuing around them like the other two mouldings. Notice it carefully, and you will see that the shape changes between one side and the other. Even in Fig. 33 you can see that the moulding on the right is a standard-shaped cornice, and it continues all the way round the choir to the same spot on the northern side. But on the left the slope is steeper, the edge altogether thinner, and the double roll-mould underneath is much longer.

It is identical to the drip mould under the nave sill! And not only that, if you extend the line of the sloping face towards the window, it meets the glass at the sill line. This moulding to the left of the sanctuary is a continuation of the one in the nave, in preparation for the same sort of steeply sloping watershed as was used there. The junction between the work of the contractor responsible for the sills and the next one lies at this buttress. The first contractor was Ruby, and in the nave he continued the sills to their full height from drip to bottom of window. But in the choir the work was at a lower level, and he only reached the first course with the drip when he had to quit the job.

His successor Scarlet had no interest in steep sloping watersheds like these. He needed a vertical wall to support a walkway that would give his men access to the glass. Finding Ruby's drip mould on one side of the buttress, he continued the motif to the east, but with a

33 The lower cornice just above the round arched openings into the crypt changes shape at the buttress. The one on the left would have repeated the arrangement of sills found in the nave.

different shape to suit its new function as a decorative item, and above it he built three courses of walling before he too left. On the inside there are some small changes in the shafts and to the heights of the coursing which confirm that the junctions occur just here.

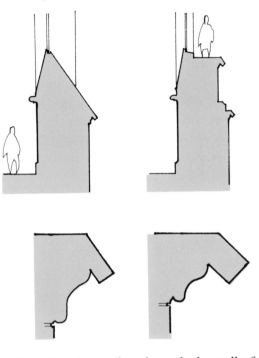

34 Sections through the walls of the nave and the sanctuary, and through the two cornices used around the eastern end. The left hand drip matches the nave.

Examine the section through the wall of the nave. Some 3 metres above the floor there is a horizontal string course. Immediately above that the wall begins to slope up to the window and forms the recess that established its width. The decision to put single windows in the nave is thus Ruby's, along with the string course and the sill. The decision to double up on the windows of the sanctuary would also have been made just above the string course. The drawing shows where Ruby and Scarlet had left and that the eastern string course is not by either of them. It is the work of Bronze, and in the next course he began the sloping recesses up to the windows, and with it permanently incorporated his decision to double them. There was nothing either Scarlet or Bronze could do to alter the nave, for all the critical decisions had already been taken under Ruby. In the choir, Scarlet probably intended to place his walkway on the inside of the glass as at Reims, but although he had determined to have a walkway, its final location was not to be his choice either. Neither walkway may have suited

Bronze, but Scarlet's continuation of the wall committed him to it, and he placed it on the outside.

Similarly, right through the building, decisions made long before the element itself had been reached were binding upon successive generations of masters. The walkway became inevitable from the moment Scarlet changed Ruby's moulding and laid up the next courses of walling, and so was the double window from the string course upwards. Even though Bronze did not lay the sill which began the openings for the glazing, he heralded it in the recesses formed for the sloping faces on the inside.

When we study the building layer by layer, the different decisions follow an orderly sequence. Even if to our eyes it seems bizarre that such big changes could be made by each contractor, we can at least see how it was done. The messiness begins to reveal the real story. The building itself gives the facts. Once they are understood, we have no choice but to accept them. We can interpret them and thus acquire a truer and deeper understanding of the period, but there is no point in denying them because they may not suit the ideas we have on how a building ought to be built. The facts come first.

This sensitivity to the stones themselves is particularly important among the flyers. Scarlet was again working on the site when the arches in the nave were laid up. He made them one-tenth of the bay thick, and you can follow his work upwards to include the bottom four or five courses over the springing, including the bases for the first columnar spokes. But in the east he was working somewhat lower down, placing the sills under the windows and the cornice of the walkway.

He began the arches at their springing with the same width as those in the nave. But he was succeeded by Ruby who built the rest of the buttress and placed the first of the voussoirs of the flyer arches. He reduced the width just above the spring with a small moulding, to just two of his English feet, which made it almost 100 mm thinner than the nave. He was not able to alter anything at the west, as he was only continuing arches and spokes already defined in Scarlet's earlier work.

The next master to make a major change to the choir was Cobalt. In the nave the heavy column spokes had been set up with round arches over them, and his only contribution was to design and place the coping over the top arch with its little roll-mould along the ridge. But in the

east where the work was somewhat slower due to the double span of the flyers over the two bays of the aisles, he was able to design the gusset in the bottom corner and the first spokes that rested against it. It was Cobalt who decided that they had no structural value whatsoever, and so he made them what they were, a screen.

In other buildings where the flyers have spokes, they are set vertically. The radiating system at Chartres is unique, and was possibly never repeated because it was more difficult to erect as each spoke had to be separately supported at the desired angle until it was pinned into the arches. Vertical ones were easier to put up as they would more or less stand on their own. By placing the choir spokes radially, Cobalt maintained a certain harmony with the nave. Was this as far as architectural unity had to be taken? Was this all the conformity that was needed, beyond which everything could be allowed to look after itself?

Today architects detail every part of a building down to the smallest bit, believing that only if their authority extends into every cranny will the building be good enough. Even though each contractor exercised an equal direction over all parts of his work, it would seem that for the client and for the permanent architect—if there was one—overall control was a decidedly less momentous issue.

If Chartres had been built in another age, the control over the builders would have been greater, and the many complications that have permitted us to see into the history of its construction would have been lost. As it is, we can divide the major part of the work up to the completion of the vaults into over thirty campaigns, carried out by only nine contractors. They each appeared for a short time, laying on average a mere three courses of masonry in each program. Some returned to the works many times and, when not there, would have found work on the other great cathedrals and abbeys round Paris, sometimes as far away as Auxerre and St Quentin. They were itinerant men, wanderers like strolling players and freelance soldiers, who moved with their chattels from place to place working where and for as long as they were needed, and packing their bags and moving on when the need had passed, or the funds to pay them had run out.

They traversed the countryside, the master and his men, possibly taking their families with them, travelling in carts large enough to be home as well as transport. Experts at their trade, they had to be where the work was, not where their hearts lay. We know little of their

35 The flyers of the choir looking through one of the trefoils in the gussets created by Cobalt a few years later than Scarlet's work in the nave.

conditions, and less of their daily lives. But from the splendid mess in Chartres we can glimpse something of them.

Each contractor may have been based on a major quarry, perhaps with dozens of gangs living in the area and accepting the direction of one master. When an addition was required to a parish church one or two gangs may have been directed to do the work, and when a huge task was ordered a dozen or more gangs may have been sent out. Some especially skilled men may have travelled only occasionally when there was sculpture or capitals to carve. With many jobs to run simultaneously, the master would not have been present all the time, for once his templets had been issued the foreman could direct the work himself. It may not be unreasonable to see the quarries as the base for these men, who left as necessary, and came home whenever possible—but in truth we know nothing of this. Beyond one certain conclusion, all is conjecture: that is that work by the same men, masters and carvers, is to be found across the landscape of northern France.

Building work was done quickly, in spite of their discontinuous contracting system, for the bulk of the cathedral was completed in some three decades. However, the final touches took almost as long again, and from the first stones in the foundations to the gables and uppermost parts of the towers almost a century later there are fully sixty-four distinguishable programs of construction. It may be disquieting to think of so many layers of work without what we would call adequate supervision, and perplexing to hear that such a manifestly wonderful building could have been created in this way.

4
DATING BY POETRY

IF WE CAN isolate so many campaigns, can we date them with equal precision? There are quite a lot of documents that survive from those years; but as with many things left us from so long ago, the selection is random. No one with an eye on the future went through the archives to put the most important to one side. Fire, revolution and war are not so selective. There is one text dated 1208, about a plumber, but no mention of what he was doing. Another notes that the procurator Robert of Blevia gave £25 for a pier, but the writer gave neither the year of the gift nor the pier concerned. Among the many like this there is sadly not one mention of a builder or a master mason before 1250.

This information may have been expunged from the record in 1389 when the so-called *Vieille Chronique* was compiled. This was a forgery, in which the author set out to move the age of the building back several centuries so as to establish the primacy of Chartres among the many French cathedrals dedicated to the Virgin. There is no mention in the *Chronique* of the fire of 1194 or of the subsequent rebuilding. The entire rebuilding program that had begun two hundred years before was forgotten, and in its place the author insists that our cathedral was the one built by Bishop Fulbert after 1020. As Simson wrote:

> The chronicler's authority was considerable. The legends he told were accepted as truth, and gradually all memories of the incomparable endeavor that had produced the present cathedral were silenced. One wonders if the oblivion into which the masters of Chartres has passed is altogether unconnected with his forgery. Whoever concocted it was certainly in a position that allowed him to destroy documents that contradicted his thesis. He actually did erase the memory of the fire of 1194 from the poem known as *The Miracles of the Blessed Virgin*. (1964, p. 226)

Scholars of the nineteenth century discovered that the *Chronique* was a forgery, and without their efforts to rectify the situation, our present understanding of the evolution of Gothic and the considerable part Chartres played in this would have been impossible. *The Miracles of the Blessed Virgin* had been transcribed into poetry from an earlier text of about 1200, now lost, and an unexpurgated copy was fortunately discovered in the neighbouring abbey of Vaux-de-Cernai, untouched by the forger. It gives the exact date of the fire, and describes the enormous damage it caused both to the old cathedral and to the town.

We read that people's grief at the personal loss of houses and property was overshadowed by the universal dismay at the total devastation of the cathedral, and apparently of the precious relics it contained. The Virgin's Tunic was the most important of these, which

> the people of Chartres had long looked upon as their shield against all perils. In 911, when the Norman Rollo beseiged Chartres, Bishop Gaucelinus had mounted the city gate and, displaying the *Sancta camisia*, had thrown the terrible Norman warriors into panic and flight. Two centuries later in 1119, the relic, carried in solemn procession by the clergy and people, had moved Louis VI, then at war with Thibault of Chartres, to spare the city. The disaster of 1194, which seemed to have destroyed the relic as well as the sanctuary, was generally looked upon as a sign of divine wrath. Because of the sins of the people, the Virgin had abandoned her shrine. The first reaction, significantly enough, was that it would be futile to rebuild either the basilica or the town. With the destruction of the cathedral, the numinous power to which Chartres owed its prosperity, its security, and indeed its existence seems to have departed. (Simson, 1964, pp. 161–2)

At this time Cardinal Melior of Pisa happened to be in the city. He personally restored the confidence of the Chapter and convinced them that the only adequate answer to the calamity was to rebuild the cathedral totally. He was so successful that the bishop and Chapter decided to commit a large part of their revenues for the next three years to the rebuilding. He followed this by ordering a meeting of all the townsfolk, and so moved them with his eloquence that he brought tears to their eyes. It was at this very moment that the bishop and the

Chapter happily appeared on the scene carrying, in great joy and wonder, the Sacred Tunic itself. It had survived by being rushed into the crypt by two priests who were on vigil that night. Its appearance at this opportune moment tipped the scales, and the people's temper was dramatically changed. They all with one accord dedicated themselves to the rebuilding of the great sanctuary, promising that it should be finer than ever before, and should be the Virgin's greatest shrine in Christendom.

The instantaneous change in people's opinion from despair to joy may seem strange, considering the destruction of both cathedral and town, but in the spirit of the times they had accepted the preservation of her relic as a sign that Mary still intended Chartres to be her especial home, and that they were to rebuild it as the palace of an empress.

Never forget that the emotional intensity of the middle ages was much greater than ours, and that they believed they were in immediate and continuous touch with the Divine. Their sudden commitment to the new work and the prodigious efforts that followed can only be understood in these terms. Their veneration of the saints and their relics, their belief in miracles and the Virgin's direct intervention in the fire show their passionate conviction that the other world was as real as our own. Heaven and earth were closer in those days.

So here in a poem is preserved the date of the fire, and curiously from another poem comes the only firm indication we have for the completion of the cathedral. Some time between 1218 and 1224 Philippe le Breton composed a valedictory piece dedicated to the French king, in which he wrote:

> It happened that not long after this,
> the Virgin Mother of God, who teaches by word and deed
>   that she is mistress of Chartres,
> desiring that the church which she called her very own
>   be restored specifically for Him with more praiseworthy
>   adornment,
> provided Vulcan with a singular opportunity
>   and allowed him to rage at will against it,
> so that there might occur a salutary burning off of the malady
>   under which this house of the Lord lay prostrate,
> and this destruction might furnish an excuse for
>   the succeeding structure

36 The vaults of the nave.

next to which none in the world gleams so brilliantly this day.
Springing up anew, now finished in its entirety
    beneath elegant vaults of cut stone,
it fears harm from no fire 'til Judgment Day;
and salvation from that fire appears to many
    through whose aid the renewed work was brought about.

(Branner, 1969, pp. 96–7)

At some time within these six years the high vaults, or at least a large part of them, must have been completed. A mere thirty years from the fire to the vaults must be considered a very short construction period indeed. We are used to thinking of mediaeval buildings being created in centuries rather than in decades. This is true enough in a way, but often work was done in a series of campaigns spread over the centuries, each one lasting a decade or two, and separated by many years during which there would be no more than routine maintenance work. A transept would be added at one time, the clerestory raised at another, and so on. Certainly towards the end of the middle ages construction was often very slow. For example during the 1400s a dozen or so men were employed for forty-six years to erect a mere two and a half bays of the nave at Troyes. But the stupendous achievement of building this cathedral in thirty years is quite in keeping with the times, for around 1200 there was an enormous amount of construction going on. Wherever we look in northern France there are buildings which date from these years. It is as if there had been a boom in the construction industry, with churches, castles, city walls, abbeys and new towns being put up pell-mell all over the countryside.

Some of the other texts from Chartres confirm the dates given in the poem without adding greatly to our knowledge. For example there is the 1221 charter describing the seating in the new choir stalls. We cannot conclude from this that the high vaults over them had necessarily been completed by then, as the stalls could have been built beneath a temporary roof at the level of the clerestory walkway.

There is another from 1198 concerning a pilgrim who was unable to reach the altar of St Laurence to leave a gift, for the crowd around it was too dense. It was thought at one time that this would date the chapel in which that altar was placed. However, we cannot justify such a precise interpretation, as the eastern end of the old church could have had stone vaults over the apse instead of timber and, not being so badly

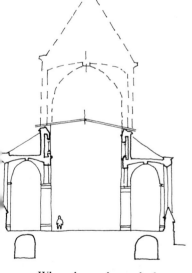

37 When the works reached the level of the clerestory walkway in 1211 a temporary roof would have been built over the nave.

damaged in the fire, may have been left standing for a few years while the builders worked on the surrounding foundation walls. Alternatively the altar could have been moved into the crypt, or they could have built temporary shelters over the old altars even if the building had been demolished, and allowed pilgrims in when the builders were not working there, or on Sundays and feast days. So that story, too, does not help us to date the building.

The text of 1210 describes a fracas between some people in the town and the clergy in which one of the priests was hit, and has been used to date parts of the cathedral. The Chapter excommunicated the town, and with the ringing of bells issued a fulmination from the pulpit. The dispute was serious enough for King Philippe-Auguste to make the three-day journey down from Paris to resolve it. Though France was the most populous country in Europe at that time, it shows how close and personal were justice and administration. The king came himself. He did not send a messenger or a judge. His writ was direct and immediate. He stood on the steps of the cathedral, judged in favour of the clergy, and made the culprit do public penance that was more humiliating than painful, and apparently effective—for we do not hear of any more violence in the town for some time.

So historians have asked which pulpit did the priest stand in, and under what roof and which steps? The document does not say. The axonometrics show that all of the major steps could have been completed, at least in part, by 1210, and the pulpit could have been placed many years before that under an earlier temporary roof that would have covered most of the building at the level of the window-sills. So even here we are no closer to a dating.

Some documents have been misread, causing endless problems, not least of which have been the oft-repeated theories about the adding of porches, the later cutting in of doorways and moving out of whole bays that have bedevilled our appreciation of the building. There is the text of 1224 in which the money changers were moved from the porch to the cloister 'so that all the dues from the stalls . . . might belong to the Chapter'. Early in this century these words were interpreted to mean that the money changers were moved so that the southern porch could be added to the transept wall. From this it followed that the sculpture of the piers could be dated a little later, and as some of them are similar to others on the west front of Notre-Dame in Paris, the latter were dated a little earlier, about 1220. Three generations of scholars have now accepted these dates, and a considerable amount of research and theorising has by now been based on them.

From Chartres and Paris most other French sculpture has been dated by style, as being either more archaic and Romanesque, and therefore earlier, or more realistic and therefore later than that at Chartres. The problems have not stopped here, for scholars have used this chronology of the sculpture to date other buildings by their carving. So the ripples from this interpretation have spread far and wide.

When it was realised some years ago that the interpretation of the 1224 document was wrong, scholars attempted to keep the chronology of the sculpture by rewriting the history of the building. For example, by style, the side doors on the north could be placed some years after the central door, and so without any other evidence whatsoever it was suggested that the north had been built with only one door, and that the other two had been cut through later. After a while these theories gave the impression that the cathedral had been built of plasticine, so easily was it supposed to have been pushed about.

But it can be shown quite clearly from the stones of the building itself that the three northern doors and the three southern ones, as well as both porches, were constructed with the rest of the work around it, and that nothing was cut in or added at a later date. The clearest place for me to explain how this sort of analysis is made is over the south porch, but the same methods can be applied throughout. First look at the gallery of kings above the porch. The argument here was that some time after the transept wall had been raised to at least the height of the clerestory, the porch was added with its lintels and the kings over them. To do that the buttresses would have been cut back, both under the statues to support the lintels, and along the sides to form the recesses for the kings.

Thick masonry elements such as buttresses were usually built from two relatively thin skins of ashlar, and in between the space was filled with rubble and mortar. This would have been a cheap technique in Chartres, for the chalk on which the cathedral stands makes an excellent mortar. It could have been mined near by and, with the flints embedded in it, lifted straight up and into the walls to form a hard-setting concrete-like core. This core would have been exposed in forming the recesses for the kings, and would have had to be refaced. Now in nearly all mediaeval building the coursing heights from one campaign will be different to those from another. This is not only true

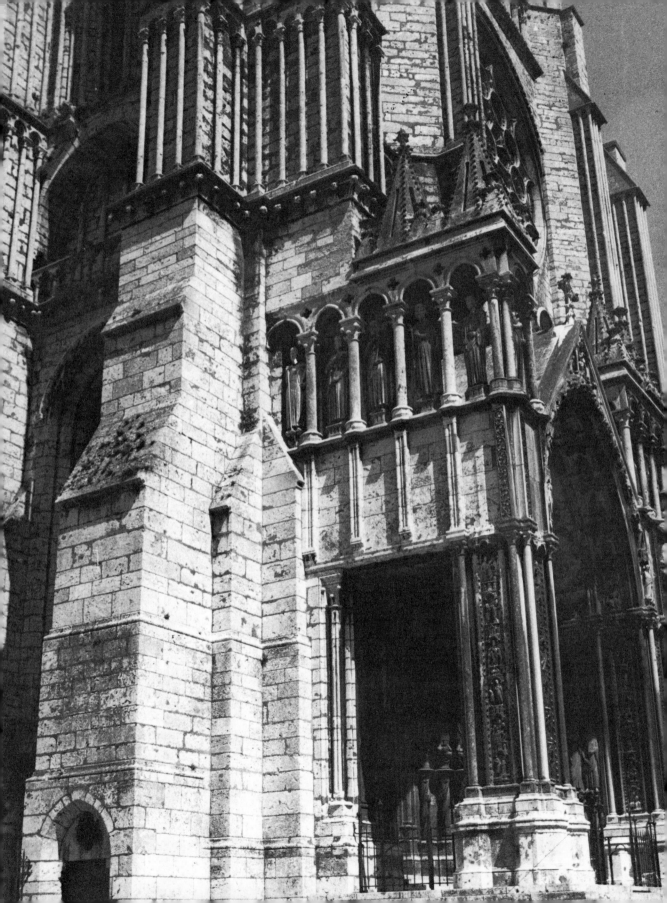

38 (*left*) The west side of the south porch showing the gallery of kings which rests over the lintels and supports the buttress above.

39 The gallery of kings over the western lintel of the south porch, with two of the continuous courses shaded.

where one wing is added to another, but is true of every one of the sixty-four campaigns found in the cathedral. Breaks or changes in construction inevitably produce visible breaks in coursing heights.

Fig. 38 shows that the coursing is continuous from the adjoining aisle wall, round both buttresses, to behind the kings, and then continues to the same heights to the east. I have shaded one of these on Fig. 39. The recesses have therefore not been refaced. Again, the arches over the columns between the kings are bedded into the buttress and support the stones above it. There are no signs of insertion or reworking, and I have also shaded one of these courses to show that it, too, is continuous.

More positive proof comes from the eastern side. Observe the first king on the right. It is not standing like the others, but a *bas relief*. It is built into the wall, and all the surrounding stonework butts into it cleanly. There is no way that this could have been added. It was carved and installed with the adjoining transept stonework. As well, there are many other smaller items, both in the north and the south, around the lintels and within the embrasures, to show that the doorways were built as we see them at the one time, and that the porches were put up shortly after with the adjoining walls.

40 (*right*) The statues of the kings on the west side of the south porch are free standing. The figure on the left is King David.

41 (*far right*) The right-hand statue on the eastern side of the porch is not free standing like the others, but is a *bas relief* built into the wall.

42 A local martyr, Saint Laumer, from the Confessor's door, the eastern opening in the south.

If the porches were not added later, what then of the sculpture? It must have been put up with the porches, for the way the stones slot into one another shows quite unambiguously that there was only one way to build them. If sculpture and porches were erected with the transepts, they must be dated closer to 1200 than to 1225, and so much of the best sculpture of the Paris Basin would have been carved a full generation earlier than has been thought. It brings the masters of this great age of French sculpture closer to the splendid works of the Royal Portal which had been carved around the middle of the 1100s.

Returning to the two poems, we have a date for the fire and a short range of dates for the completion of 'the elegant vaults'. It therefore took between twenty-five and thirty-one years to construct the cathedral. It was tempting to count the number of building campaigns that lay between the start of the work and the stripping of the formwork and plastering of the first vaults over the nave. There are just thirty campaigns, and after that just an extra two to complete the vaults in the choir. They match up, there being almost the same number of years as there were campaigns. The simple solution was to give these campaigns an annual dating, even though there would be errors. On the whole the errors would be minuscule in the earlier years, and in the later ones would probably not be more than a year or two out. Even where some small campaigns may have lasted only a few months, while the larger would have gone on for years, the overall picture would be reasonably accurate. Indeed never before have we had such accurate dating for each part of a great early French building. We can now say with only slight error that this part, this course, and even this stone was laid in this or that particular year.

There are even small pieces of corroborative evidence, too. For example, when the local count, Louis, went to the Crusades in 1204 he joined in the sack of Constantinople, and in the looting that followed obtained the head of St Anne, mother of the Virgin. In the next year, according to our year-by-year chronology, the trumeau with the figure of Anne was carved and put under the lintel of the central northern door. In 1208 Roger the plumber was mentioned for the first time, and in the next year he would have been laying the lead sheeting over the roofs of the aisles.

When the king came to the town to resolve the conflict between the clergy and some of the more boisterous locals, he could have stood on any of the steps, north, south or west, as they were all in use by 1210.

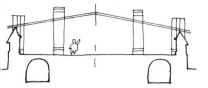

43 The whole church could have been opened to public worship by 1203 with a lightweight roof discharging the rainwater over the aisle sills.

The pulpit from which the priest fulminated against the town may be placed where it suits you, as by then the entire cathedral could have been opened for worship under a temporary roof.

Admittedly this roof would have been set only at the height of the aisle sills, but even that would have given a clear space under the ceiling of 4.5 m, and possibly much more at the centre. Temporary roofs were quite common in those days. Fairs would be set up overnight under acres of canvas and hide, making lightweight structures that were reasonably waterproof, easy to put up and quick to remove. The same used over the cathedral would have allowed the clergy to move into the nave in 1200, and to expand into the choir three years later. The southern doors could have been opened in 1206, and the special preparations made so that the north-eastern door could be opened in 1204 show that by then most of the cathedral was in use. After all, if money was to be raised for the works, how were people to be encouraged to give it if all services had to be held in a barn for thirty years? The priests and pilgrims alike would want to get into the building as quickly as possible to set up the altars and to continue their rites without delay. Not to be able to pray to their saints and relics would have been a far worse deprivation than the inconvenience of a low ceiling or a bit of damp.

The first datable donation for the glass, Chancellor Berou's gift for one of the choir clerestory windows by the crossing, is within one year of the earliest date in which a templet could have been made from the opening itself. And the precise document of 1221 apportioning the seats in the new choir stalls works in particularly well. By 1215 the temporary roof could have been raised to the level of the clerestory walkway, opening the aisles and the triforium to their full height for the first time. The space underneath would have been clear of scaffolding, and the stone *jubé* that divided the clergy's portion of the choir from the nave could have been begun under it. The small evidence we have from the few remaining stones of the *jubé*, wantonly pulled out and buried under the paving in the 1700s, shows that at least four of the contractors working elsewhere in the cathedral had a hand in it, and that the only years in which they could have together done the parts the details suggest would be between 1217 and 1220. This would not be an unreasonable time to construct such a delicate and complex screen with all of its sculpture, and so it would have been ready for the clergy's occupation in the next year.

Annual dating does not mean that the men worked in the summer and went away each winter, though work normally slowed down during the darker months. Their winters were not particularly severe, nor were they as harsh as they were to become in the next century. The weather was changing around 1200, as it is today, but climatically Chartres was built during those splendid fertile seasons with which France had been blessed for some centuries past, and which had made her the most populous and richest country in Europe.

There is nothing explicit in the texts to tell us why the masters came and went. It could not have been lack of confidence in the builders, for the Chapter kept on re-engaging the same men under the same masters time after time, which would not have happened to anyone sacked for negligence or incompetence. However, there are hints from Durham, Westminster and Laon that the rate of work was dependent on finance, and that when the money ran out the work had to stop. At Chartres the poet who described the fire wrote that at one stage 'all finances suddenly gave out, so that the supervisors had no wages for the workmen, nor did they have in view anything that could be given otherwise.' (Branner, 1969, p. 99)

There were no fiduciary issues in the early middle ages, no ways to raise money by bonds or promissory notes. There was either cash, be it money or precious objects, or loans at staggering rates of interest. There was no forward budgeting either, just faith. These enormous projects were begun without any idea at all of what the costs would be, but just the confident expectation that somehow God would provide and they would be met. Under these conditions is it any wonder that the treasury was often empty? We find the same layered construction in many parts of Europe, in Norman England and southern Italy for example, as well as around the Paris Basin. Rapid turnover seems to be particularly associated with booming building conditions, when the teams were growing into great organisations that were building so fast that they were constantly threatening to outstrip available funds. They built themselves out of a job, so to speak, and were thus compelled to move elsewhere.

These annual layers at Chartres, now so neatly dated, show us that the nave vaults would have been finished in 1223, and the ones in the choir in 1225. Both of these suit the second poem, which was written some time between 1218 at the earliest and 1224. Bronze's double windows in the sanctuary would then be 1201, the exquisite Scarlet corbels in the triforium would be 1209, and Ruby reduced the width of the choir flyer arches in 1216. In the transept doorways we find that nearly all the sculpture was in place by 1203 and that the first pieces would have had to be carved within three years of the fire.

This sort of precision is very exciting indeed. For example, we can see how over a number of years Scarlet modified the way he designed windows. As we saw in those he designed in 1200, he used nothing but 45° triangles, but after 1206 he introduced 60° angles, and the steps in the evolution became a little more complicated. His foot unit does not change over the years, nor do his corbels, his doors, etc., but only his geometry. The same master can be found working in Laon, and there his windows follow the later geometry rather than the earlier. This may help us date that part of Laon. Similarly there is a qualitative change in Bronze's windows during the 1198 campaign, and some of his details change over this time too, like the corbel which was reduced in size. His work in the crypt of Le Mans could therefore be a little after his first campaign in Chartres.

The same annual dating system can be extended into the campaigns after 1225, though the amount of work being done in each program was diminishing once the main vaults had been finished. Each was by now so small, sometimes no more than the laying of a hundred blocks of stone each time, that you could see that the Chapter was in no hurry to finish the work. Once the major space had been enclosed, a lot of the enthusiasm that had carried them forward seems to have been lost. Maybe thirty years of unremitting effort in raising funds and handling the intricacies of a large construction site were enough even for such dedicated worshippers of their patron, the Virgin Queen.

Chartres still had to suffer from another fire, which, like that of 1194, began within the roof of the cathedral. It burnt one windy night in 1836 and destroyed the entire thirteenth-century wooden roof, and melted the lead that covered it. Le Breton's words that the new cathedral 'beneath elegant vaults of cut stone fears no harm from fire 'til Judgment Day' came true. Though the roof burnt, the stonework stayed firm, and nothing below the vaults was damaged by the flames. The masters of the thirteenth century had indeed built well.

The new roof was erected in four years, with a cast-iron frame. It was covered in copper, and gives Chartres the green effect it has today, though we should remember that the original roof was lead lined and, like the rest of the building, would have been grey all over. To commemorate the fact, a cast-iron plaque was made and fixed to the inside of the west wall, within the roof space. It gives the names of the architects and the date, and the names of the contractor and the fabricator of the cast iron.

But already it is hard to read. The letters have lost their crispness in the damp air, and it will not be long before parts become altogether illegible. This has happened in less than 150 years. What will it be like after eight centuries? Men may then see the roof, and marvel, but will have as little evidence for its date and for the men who built it as we do today for the cathedral itself. Time is the great destroyer. I suppose we must consider ourselves fortunate to have even the little information we do possess. At least we have the building, largely untouched, and the immense good fortune to possess the two poems which give Chartres the lonely distinction of being one of the few buildings from the period with any certain dates at all.

5
THE CLIENT

WITH THE BUILDERS coming and going like migrating birds, someone must have been answerable to the clergy. Normally the Chapter appointed a permanent supervisor to control the builders and to pay them. He would have found the contractors each time, engaged them, and seen to it that they performed. He checked their accounts, agreed with the wages paid and supervised the administrative side of the works. Some of these things may also have been done by the master in charge of the crews, but the final responsibility for many of them lay with the client.

However, considering the number of building campaigns and contractors involved, one would think there should also have been an architect, someone to have some sort of control over the vagaries of the builders, and to guide them towards a single artistic design. In spite of the many alterations, large and petty, that the contractors introduced in each campaign, there is still an underlying and often superb cohesiveness about the cathedral that makes it difficult to believe that it would have been built without some permanent architectural guidance.

In theory the roles of client and architect are separable and distinguishable. But in practice this is not so. Some clients wish to be more involved than others, and some have over the years acquired a considerable proficiency in administering building works and have learnt a lot about the trade from dealing with professionals. However, we can separate some of the client's decisions from the others, which will be an important step in helping to resolve the more difficult problem of the architect. His role we shall discuss later.

There was bound to be a constant interchange of ideas between the Chapter and the masters, and as ideas could have come from either, the client's role could have been a large one. For example, the doubling of the windows in the sanctuary could have been requested by the client. Someone may have seen another building, or even a model for one with such a glass wall, liked it, and sold the idea to Chapter and master alike. This would not affect the arguments in chapter 2, for no matter where ideas may have come from, the masters would have carried them out in their own way, and to their own rules. So while the changes tell us a lot about the builders, they tell us nothing about the source of the ideas they used.

On the whole I am inclined to think that the clergy would have followed the ruling given at the Council of Nicea that 'the arrangement belongs to the clergy, and the execution to the artist', so that in general the church's involvement in the detailing and structural problems would have been minimal. But in certain things the client is the expert, and this is usually where we find his major influence. The most important would have been in the form of the cathedral, the arrangement of the chapels and transepts, the size of the choir, and so on. These are functional things, and we all expect the client to tell us what he wants, and preferably in great detail. But even with sophisticated clients the architect often has to write the brief for him. A client should know what he wants, but not having the experience he seldom has enough faith in his ideas to follow them through to a solution. He lacks the architect's expertise and his familiarity with other possible solutions.

In the middle ages people did not see that function was the only attribute required of a building. Beyond the events and needs of our world lay whole hierarchies of other beings and existences. This is not something we readily understand today, for where science provides the answers there are no mysteries. They believed that behind the superficial appearance of things lay a greater reality that would, if only it could be tapped, reveal the true nature of the universe. The ultimate mystery was as real to them as the laws of nature are to us. They not only tried to find ways to understand them, but, as we do with scientific discoveries, attempted to apply what they had learnt to what they did. The results of their investigations were expressed in numbers and in geometry, not unlike our formulae. They were applied to buildings so that the structure would reflect the Divine, and, by reflecting it, illuminate man's way. We shall discuss this more in the next chapter, but the plan would be the most obvious place for us to look for the influence of the client.

The second would be in the messages, or what is called iconography, of the glass and sculpture. The arrangement would certainly have been discussed by the clergy, and we can see evidence for delays in the work that were probably caused by their vacillation in approving the arrangement of the sculpture. The design of the southern doors seems to have provided few problems, for the figures were begun as early as 1197, and they were the first to be finished. The arrangement is impeccable and predictable. The apostles stand below the Last Judgment, and are flanked by the martyrs and the confessors who indicate the two roads to salvation: the least difficult being to die for the cause, and the more demanding being daily to follow the teachings of the church fathers. Marvellous as some of the individual pieces are, it is on the whole a somewhat straightforward and conventional grouping.

On the north side, the eastern door dates from the same time as the southern ones, and is also conventional. The most powerful and well integrated of the iconographies is that of the central northern door. The earliest piece of sculpture dates from 1202, whereas the eastern door next to it had not only been started four years earlier, but was sufficiently advanced by the next year to be opened to the public. This suggests that the central door had been delayed, and I presume this was while the clergy argued about the subtleties of the arrangement.

Its iconography hinges upon the dedication of the cathedral, which was to the bodily Assumption of the Virgin. This was not officially accepted doctrine at the time, though it was generally believed to be true. Chartres owed much of its pre-eminence to the fact that it was not just dedicated to the Virgin, as were so many other great buildings, but to her actual presence next to God, almost as a divinity in her own right. The tympanum and lintels show her death, resurrection and crowning in Heaven. The huge figures in the embrasures depict the kings and prophets who prefigure Christ's coming and who are either Mary's ancestors or who knew her while Christ was alive. The list naturally begins with David, though this was not the first David to be carved for this door. There is an earlier figure of him, now hidden among the kings over the south porch (shown in Fig. 40), and presumably rejected in favour of the present one. The stance of the older figure follows the standard pattern, where David holds the lyre and is supported by the tree of Jesse.

The David in the doorway is far more complex, and more

interesting. He no longer holds his symbol, the lyre, but the crown of thorns and the nails, the symbols of Christ. The whole tone of the entry has been changed. The great figures no longer represent just the lineage, but have in addition acquired the aspects of Jesus himself. Samuel prepares to slaughter the lamb, symbolising the sacrifice of Christ on the Cross. Abraham offers his son Isaac in the way that God offered His. And in the outer figures Melchizedek holds the symbols of the Eucharist as the first king to be a priest, while on the right stands Peter as the first priest to be made king as head of the church. The interconnections continue, becoming deeper and more compelling. We are moved by them at many levels, and become increasingly aware of the timbre of the whole of these constantly overlapping connections. It is a great doorway, which clearly took a lot of discussion and argument to prepare. Here the clergy used their abilities to the best. It shows a touch of the Chapter's earlier reputation as the centre of French learning, now taken over by the new schools of Paris.

The last door to be arranged was the next one to the west, the famous Job doorway. The iconography is unusual, if not unique. Examination of the near-by staircase and the walls that surround it shows that construction on this part of the building had been frozen for some eight years. The consequences were serious and expensive. While the doorway and the outer face of the surrounding walls was halted at the level of the porch lintels, the interior had to be continued much higher to support the adjoining arch of the arcades.

To make this clearer, examine the section through the north transept, looking westwards from the choir side. The date is 1207. On the left the crossing pier is much higher than anything else, and the walls of the near-by attic rooms have just been set out by Cobalt. The vault in the second aisle bay had been completed the year before, followed by the arcade arch in the third bay, so that the formwork under the vault could be struck. On the right this arch is supported on the inner skin of the transept wall, but observe the stratagems! It was possible to raise the inner face almost 3.5 m above the outside because this wall is almost 2.5 m thick, and the difference could be absorbed within the staircase, shown passing through the wall.

When the work was frozen, the door embrasures had been built to the course immediately underneath the capitals over the statues. The capitals are carved on quite large blocks which are set deeply into the wall, because they are the sole support for the big statues themselves.

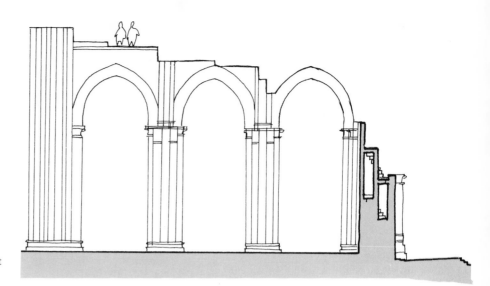

44 Section through the north transept looking west. It is 1207, and Cobalt has just erected the arch in the third bay, with some difficult manoeuvres to provide support at the outside.

As the work stopped here, it is a fair guess that the statues had not yet been carved, and the builder had to wait for them before proceeding. Why otherwise stop the work here, and force himself to put up with all the difficulties it caused on the inside?

Immediately above the capitals there is a continuous moulding that ties them together, and on that rests both the statues within the archivaults and the lintels of the porch. Hence the delay in the statues had ramifications in all directions. The hole left in the wall was not just the size of the door, but fanned outwards all around it. Normally when faced with a building problem, a mason will produce a building answer, be it aesthetic or not, just so that he can get on with the work. So something must have been holding him back, and my guess is that it was the Chapter. It was their prerogative to arrange the iconography of the sculpture, and for some reason they were not doing it, though I can imagine the master pleading with them to do so.

It is significant that the first statues carved for this doorway, including the story of Job from which it gets its name, date from 1207–8, and that it was just at this time that a new Chancellor was appointed. He was Pierre de Roissy, famous in history as a resolute hunter of heretics, and as the author of a treatise on, of all things, the Book of Job. In this, as Katzenellenbogen explains (p. 58): 'he interpreted Job, as St. Gregory had done before, as both Christ and Church. It certainly seems possible that he suggested the representation of Job's suffering as a suitable reminder of the dangers to which the church was exposed in his own time', from the Cathar and

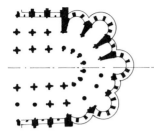

45 The choir: above, as it was planned; below, as it was built, with a double ambulatory.

other heresies. When Pierre was appointed, he may first have had to decide the subject for this doorway, and order the master to proceed with the sculpture.

It is a remarkable tribute to the masters' efficiency and ingenuity that not only were they able to proceed with the rest of the building in spite of the difficulties, but once the problems were resolved they were able to fill in the hole and be almost back to normal within a few years. The sutures are hard to notice today.

The results of another decision by the client were even less fortunate. The archaeological evidence shows that in the first plan for the cathedral the eastern end had been laid out for a single ambulatory, with seven chapels radiating off it, and two additional ones at the ends of the outer sanctuary aisles. Everyone was working towards this until 1199, when the clergy made the momentous, and in my opinion disastrous, decision to alter it. There is a document preserved from the year before that may show us something of their state of mind.

Remember that in the twelfth century Chartres was primarily a pilgrimage church, and that every year many thousands of folk came from all over France, indeed from all over the Christian world, to pray at the most important and efficacious shrine of the Virgin. The text relates how one pilgrim, wishing to leave a donation of money on one of the altars, found that no matter how hard he tried, his way was constantly barred by an immense crowd of fellow pilgrims who had got there before him. After trying with all his might he left and, walking home, had to spend the night in a field. When he woke in the morning he found he had been robbed. He dashed back to the cathedral, perhaps to pray for forgiveness, or perhaps just to complain— mediaeval documents are generally uncritical of motives. When he arrived he still could not get near the altar, but to his amazement there, resting on top of the table, lay his purse—a miracle!

However, note the crowd in this story. Too many people were trying to get to the altars. Did the prospect of an ever-increasing flood of worshippers frighten the clergy? More and more of them coming into what was to become one of the largest churches in Christendom, and still there might not be room enough? It must have seemed like the nightmare of the sorcerer's apprentice. The clergy may have panicked, and determined even at this late stage that they needed more processional and general milling space. So they ordered the master to redesign the choir, and to double up on the ambulatory.

None of the internal walls had yet been begun, though the outside of the work had been brought some 5 m above the ground and was just about to rise above the level of the floor. The change could still be done without having to demolish anything, but the consequences were far from happy. The two chapels at the end of the sanctuary disappeared altogether, and four of the seven in the apse retreated into being mere recesses off the ambulatory.

More important, the centres of the western chapels had to be moved to the west, which altered the entire arrangement of mullions and windows. Architecturally the result was appalling. Stone piers sit over the windows of the crypt, and though we can handle this sort of thing structurally, it looks bad, as can be seen in Fig. 7. And where the western pair of chapels met the first buttresses, they overhung the foundation walls and had to be supported on complex corbelling, which can be seen in Fig. 33. Because the centres were moved, the buttresses between them which were to support the clerestory flyers were moved too, so that none of the rondpoint axes was straight any more. The confusion in these bays is too great for pleasure. It may have been the practical thing to do, but architecturally it was pretty unfortunate.

On the other hand the Chapter were punctilious in compelling each master to follow the same arrangement for the interior. There are slight changes between the building programs, but in general the eastern end is just like the west; the arcades are the same height, the vaults have the same ribs and the same spurred bosses, and the clerestory is the same, or at least is superficially the same. The clerestory windows in the choir are wider and the roses on top larger than in the nave, and their lancets are not as high. The choir triforium has five openings, while the nave has four and is a little shorter. These differences are enough to indicate the crews, but the overall uniformity, if the disorder on the outside and in other buildings is to be any guide, shows that the builders were being compelled to follow a single format. This was demanded by the client, not the architect, because it continued unchanged for over forty years, which is longer than the active life of a trained person.

The clergy may have been following a model, perhaps one prepared by the first master. None has survived from this period, though a few account rolls show they did make them, that they were often expensive, and may even have been large enough to get into. However, even if we still possessed the model, it would not look much like the

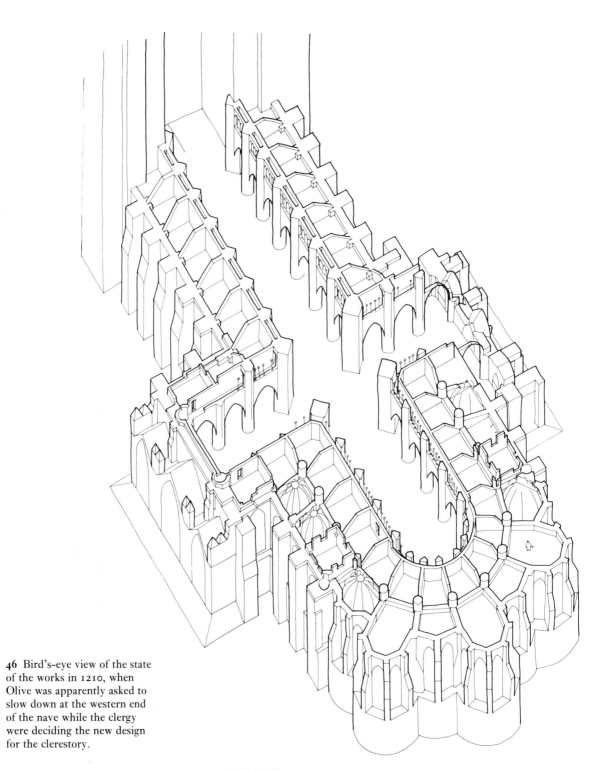

46 Bird's-eye view of the state
of the works in 1210, when
Olive was apparently asked to
slow down at the western end
of the nave while the clergy
were deciding the new design
for the clerestory.

completed building. When you spend four or more decades on a great work, both ideas and fashions change, even in sacred architecture. The model of 1194 may have been completely up to date, but it still would have been the work of one man and his time. Men and times change.

Imagine the situation today. Suppose we had begun to build in 1960 to the best ideas available, and it is going to take us well into the 1990s to complete. By the time we are half-way up or so we are going to look back at the design of the sixties with some disdain. Our lifts are faster, our air conditioning better, and we use less plain glass and more sculptured concrete. An entirely new vocabulary has been developed in the last two decades. And so it was in the middle ages, which is why the triforium and clerestory levels are usually more 'advanced' or Gothic than the aisles.

There is evidence at Chartres that one master was ordered to stop work when he reached a certain level. This was Olive in 1210 (Fig. 46). His mason's marks peter out near the ceiling of the attic rooms at the western end of the nave, level with the capping over the triforium passageway. Immediately over this lies the walkway to the clerestory, and the indents for the windows that determine its layout.

It looks as if the clergy were reconsidering the arrangement for the upper windows. The ones in the model may have been large single openings, as were so often to be found at this time and would have been one of the commonest solutions of the 1190s. The use of double windows in the sanctuary may have inspired them to think again, or they may have been aware of the contemporary work at Soissons, where the open double-lancets of the clerestory were being set up almost in the same year. This is why we have to be careful not to date the ideas in the upper parts of buildings to the foundation year. The concepts built in at any level belong to the time they were put in, and, unless something else indicates otherwise, that is all.

It was quite common in the middle ages to have competitions for architectural work, possibly more common than it is today. It would appear that when the work reached the top of the triforium the Chapter decided to reconsider the whole arrangement for the upper level of windows. They ordered the contractor to stop work when he reached the course below the clerestory, while he continued with other lower parts of the fabric. I imagine they sent messengers out to all parts of the land calling for ideas, and that many builders responded, including those who had already worked on the cathedral. They would

47 The window design which won the 1211 competition, by Ruby.

have made drawings, and perhaps even a model of a typical bay, to show off their ideas to the best advantage, and then met together with the building committee to argue their case.

What an occasion this would have been. Masters from all round the Paris Basin would have travelled slowly by horse, probably accompanied by a servant or by one of their leading hands, to congregate at Chartres. Some of the schemes would have been rejected at once, and some put aside for further thought. At last the decision was made, and it seems to have gone to Ruby, for we find his corbels and his window details and geometry in the next campaign. The

Chartres clerestory design is absolutely up to date for 1210, a superb open arrangement with twin lancets crowned with a rose (Fig. 47).

As with so many other things in Chartres, the arrangement is unique to this building. The rose is the full width of the bay, so that the arch over it is round instead of being pointed. This is typical of Ruby. He always preferred round arches over his windows and mouldings. The round arch has quite a different effect from the pointed one. It returns the eye to the building, where the other lets it fly outwards. It holds the attention within the structure, allowing it to skip horizontally from bay to bay. In all the other double-lancet clerestories in France, including the one at Soissons, the rose was reduced in size so that a pointed arch could be placed round it.

But having selected the scheme, the clergy stuck to it. Even in the last bays of the northern transept which were not completed until almost thirty years later, they insisted on the masters following the same arrangement with the big rose and the round arch. It was not that they were being deliberately old-fashioned, but that they sought then, as they had consistently throughout all the years, a certain uniformity in the interior. Old-fashioned they were not, for only a few years earlier they had commissioned one of the most advanced all-glass rose windows in the adjoining transept wall, the great northern rose of France.

In the original model, the cathedral would have had nine towers. One enormous spire would have crowned the crossing, with eight others surrounding it. The older western towers formed two, there was a pair flanking each transept, and one on each side of the apse, with that over the crossing forming the ninth. With them Chartres may have looked more like a German Rhineland church than a French Classical Gothic one. Even Reims, which we now see under a long and dominant roof, was to have been capped with a crown of spires, and at Laon five of the towers were taken quite some way above the roof before being stopped. This passion for climbing constantly higher and higher had developed over the past century. It produced buildings that may not have been as high inside as they were to become, but were so upward-soaring outside that they were like towers of Babel stretching up to the sky.

But wherever we look in the 1220s we find that taste was changing, and that the multi-fingered silhouettes that seemed to propel us into the heavens was giving way to the urbanity of simple roofs. The

48 Hypothetical reconstruction of the original scheme for the cathedral, with nine towers.

towers, if there were any, were only to be given spires at the western end, and the rest were almost always finished off at the level of the vaults. The first murmur of this new attitude at Chartres was the decision taken in 1222 to omit the crossing tower. Steep roofs were seldom used where there was a crossing tower, as the effect was spoiled, much of the tower being hidden by the roof. But, without the tower, the pitch of the roof could be raised. This increased the wind loads which, on the open plains of the Beauce, is quite an important factor. Stand on top of the building on a stormy day and you have to hang on. The winds can be quite frightening.

It was therefore decided that a third row of flyers should be added to buttress the top of the wall where it supported the roof. Do not minimise this decision. It probably cost them more than the tower they left out. Though the amount of stonework was not great, heavy dependable scaffolding had to be erected to support these arches. There would also have been some concern over the thin piers

49 The beginnings of the fourth stage of the south–east tower can just be seen alongside the turret that caps the stairs.

supporting the middle of the choir flyers, that they might not have been large enough to support the extra loads without bending. As it is, they are among the slenderest supports to be found anywhere before reinforced concrete transformed these things. Unsupported laterally for a height of 17 m, the ratio of height to width is roughly 7 : 1, which is rather dangerous in masonry.

The next set of towers to be left out were the apsidal ones, for when the southern tower almost collapsed in 1228 it was decided not to proceed with them either. This left six. They continued to work on the four over the transepts, and to repair the burnt-out spire over the northern of the two western towers, but slowly, and without enthusiasm, for almost twenty years. They got little higher than the gallery over the gables, and just before the cathedral was dedicated in 1260 by Louis IX, then an old man, the final decision was made to stop work on the transept towers too.

Gradually the original dream dissolved, and Chartres was brought into line with the new ideals current in the rest of France. By now the clergy seem to have had enough of the hard work needed to keep a big building program afloat. They felt they had other important things to do. Perhaps six decades of the noise and dust of a major work-site was enough, and they decided to draw a line through the accounts and call the cathedral finished. Personally I think that the age of religious mysticism that had produced the energy to build these cathedrals had passed, and that men had returned to the more ordinary and mundane interests that are our most common pursuits. Periods of high endeavour are hard to attain and even more difficult to maintain. The beginning of the change in this spirit can probably be marked as closely by the elimination of the crossing tower as by any other historical act we know of.

So we can see through all these examples that the role of the client was a complex one. Sometimes he kept the work abreast of the times, and at others disturbed the work and made the builder's task more difficult. Was he any different from our clients today? As the centuries passed, he continued to change the building as the need seized him. Fortunately the changes were not great, for though the diocese of Chartres was a large one, it lay off the main trade routes and was not as prosperous as some.

A small room had been built off the south side of the nave in the 1190s and in it was lodged the bellows for the near-by organ.

Thirteenth-century organs were smaller affairs than the ones we know, and the wind for them was produced by generations of sweating choirboys, conveniently hidden from view in little rooms like these. But shortly after 1400 the organ was taken out of the aisle and moved up into the triforium, and the bellows put into the attic behind. This left the downstairs room free, and on it, in the most economical way possible, Count Louis of Vendôme built the little chapel that bears his name. Fortunately this was the only chapel to be added, for the rest of the exterior has been left as it was.

Inside a lot more has been changed. One of the most damaged areas is the western end, but there are enough pieces of the old work remaining to give us a pretty good indication of what happened here. In the additions made to the Fulbert church after 1135, a three-by-three bay narthex was built between the two towers. It was vaulted, and the remains of some of the columns and the marks made by the vaults against the walls can still be seen. It was quite a low chamber, and

50 The low roof of the narthex compelled the master to make adjustments to the floor level.

supported a floor that was just below the sill of the three western lancets.

The splendid glass in these lancets survived the fire of 1194, yet the near-by walls of the towers show how fierce the flames were, quite close to them. The northern tower had a wooden spire and, as it burned, the strong westerly wind made it crash into the nave, bringing much of the stonework down with it. The glass could have survived only if it had been protected within a fire-proof chamber with a wall shielding it from the holocaust raging in the nave, and a vault to keep out falling débris. So these windows would have lit a tall room, perhaps a chapel, that was framed between the towers. After the fire the builders demolished the vault and the eastern wall of this room, and one of the bays of the narthex, leaving the western two as a lobby to protect the pilgrims on their way into the crypt.

They may have intended to keep it for no more than a few years until something more suitable could be built, but by 1200 it had been decided to retain it permanently, perhaps for the pleasant feeling of security it gave on entry, and perhaps for the gallery above that gave an uninterrupted view down the new work. For in that year they erected the first of the temporary roofs over the nave, and laid the floor. This floor is rather unusual, for it is not level, but slopes upwards from the threshold of the western doors to the main level at the fourth or fifth bay.

If other buildings are any guide to their intentions, they would not have inclined the floor like this if they had not been forced to. In the aisles it is level, for it sits immediately over the crypt vaults, but in the main part of the nave they would not have had headroom under the low vaults of the narthex had it not been lowered, as you can see in Fig. 50, which shows these bays as they were in the middle ages. The lowering of the floor exposed the footings under the piers, and, though the footings are used today as steps, you can see that this was not the intention.

Having decided to leave these two bays of the narthex in place, they tidied up the inside face of the towers by adding shafts from the floor of the gallery upwards, and by refacing the upper parts with recesses like false windows which were at one time painted in imitation of stained glass. The cathedral stayed like this until some time in the 1600s, when the clergy considered removing the organ to build a larger one against the western wall. It may seem extraordinary to us that they would have contemplated blocking out the most marvellous glass in the cathedral, but building organs at the west end was quite fashionable at the time, and the seventeenth century had far less regard for mediaeval glass than we have.

The demolition work was begun, the narthex pulled out and most of the columns were stripped from the walls. They had even begun some new mouldings and a couple of columns for the new organ gallery when work was stopped. The builders were just ordered off the job, nothing was put back and the damaged work was left, never to be made good. It still shows the scars of that misguided decision (Fig. 36).

Instead, the Chapter decided to leave the organ in the same location, and to replace it with a larger one. The only change was to remove the glass from two of the clerestory lancets which were covered by the enormous pipes required by the big sounds of the times.

About the same time as they were changing the western end of the cathedral they decided that the outside of the choir stalls was not prepossessing enough, and began to build the imposing screen with its minuscule renaissance carving and the spacious dioramas of the Life of Christ. The stalls themselves, innovative and original as they were when first occupied in 1221, were pulled out in the eighteenth century and replaced with the present tediously dull seating and the dreadful marble facing that lines the inside of the choir. At the same time, the screen between the choir and the crossing, the *jubé*, was pulled out and the bits, including some of the finest pieces of small-scale carving from the period, were just buried under the paving. As a result the tenor of the choir is much feebler than it could have been. The doubling of the ambulatory, the modernising of the screen and the appalling simplicity of the choir stalls have robbed this part of the cathedral of much of its charisma.

These gradual changes for the worse are still going on, though now the client is the State, which owns the cathedral, and the tourists, who would like to. In spite of the much careful and well-intentioned restoration the structure is subtly and insensitively damaged each year. A hole is drilled through a wall for a waterpipe that is needed in case there is another fire, but it is drilled next to the base of a column, and a corner is knocked off in the process. Scaffolding is placed against a wall so that a roof can be repaired, and repaired carefully in the old way with dowels instead of nails, but the men working there somehow damage a moulding. Worse, much worse, is the effect of the motor-car, and a short-sighted town that will not forgo some of its commercial advantages to save the building that generates them. Fumes and exhaust are corroding the statues, for the stone they are carved from is softer than the limestone of the structure, and I have personally seen a small piece of the Royal Portal fall to the ground in front of me. There are photographs of the Portal taken only thirty years ago that show fingers and hair and noses that no one will ever see again. It may not take long now for the pollution of our generation to destroy carvings that have survived weather, war, revolution and the other manifold ravages of the thirty generations before us. In this the public and the merchant have become more influential than the client, and maybe, in their common thoughtlessness, more destructive.

This pollution is like graffiti, and reflects our attitude to the world. The first scrawled signatures on the fabric are those of the men who plastered the walls of the triforium passage in the 1760s. From then on, men have had to sign their names on the ancient fabric, and though literacy was not much greater in the eighteenth century than it was in the thirteenth, the age that produced the cathedrals left no personal disfigurements on its surface.

In those years, I suppose, the client's influence on the building was more fortunate than not. He acted with insensitivity in the matter of the apse and with irresponsible procrastination over the iconography of the Job doorway. But on the other hand he chose good schemes for the clerestory windows and the sculpture of the central northern door. He consistently held to the one arrangement for the interior for two full generations, and in the midst of the disasters following the fire itself was able to so inspire the first master than he produced one of the most marvellous plans of all times, beautifully co-ordinated in number and geometry, that was to inspire all the men who worked on the cathedral over the next four decades.

6
PUTTING SIGNIFICANCE INTO FORM

I IMAGINE THAT the first meeting between the Chapter and the master may have begun with a talk by the Dean, something like this:

Welcome, Master Scarlet, to our first meeting. Following the terrible destruction of our old cathedral we wish to see it rebuilt, almost entirely. Demolish the upper church and in its place build us the most beautiful cathedral in the land. We want it to be a fit home for our patron, the Blessed Virgin. This is no ordinary job, for this is the most important of her shrines in Christendom.

The ground upon which the cathedral stands is sacred to the holy relics of the Virgin and the saints. Therefore the crypt is to be retained, and protected during the construction. The new building is to sit over it and to be the same length, so that the high altar and the chapels will remain in their usual places over the most sacred parts of the crypt.

We have in Chapter, I admit not without difficulty, resolved to retain the western towers and the portals in between them. The badly damaged upper parts of the northern tower can be rebuilt as you think fit.

However, we are unanimous in wanting the new church to be cruciform in shape, in memory of Our Lord's Passion, with transepts north and south. You will of course place doorways through them, as we want sculpture set in their embrasures. We are even now eagerly discussing the possible arrangements and have already received a promise from our Lord Count Louis to pay for the work on the great central door, that of the Judgment itself.

But we have a difficulty. During the time it takes you to put up enough of the new building for us to occupy under the usual temporary roof, what are we to do for accommodation? The crypt, large as it is, is certainly too small for all the Holy Offices and the Mission of Our Lady. We do not wish to move down there, at least not for all that time. And even if we do use it for some of our worship, how do we get in and out while you are building?

These are real problems, and we must ask you to resolve them for us in one way or another. One of our brothers has put forward the suggestion that, as the eastern end of the old church has not been damaged as much as the west, due to the stone vaults over the apse and the chapels, we could perhaps remain in occupation of that part while you begin in the nave. We could then change over when it suits.

Last, there is the arrangement of the building. Since the time of Chancellor Thierry we have given great consideration to the meanings of numbers and their significance in God's plan. We conclude that two are particularly relevant to the Blessed Virgin, and you are to incorporate them into every aspect of the new building. One is seven, for she is the patron of the seven Liberal Arts, and the other, her most precious and yet most secret number, is nine.

Though Scarlet would have understood at once what the Dean was saying to him, we today may need a short word of explanation. Seven has since time immemorial been the number of earthly cycles, as opposed to the ten heavenly cycles. It is the number of days in the week, a quarter of the period of the moon, the number of the planets, the sun and the moon. We could go on for ever, but Philo summed it up when he wrote that 'nature delights in the number seven'. Nine is more subtle, and since ancient times has been the number of the Goddess. The Virgin has been called in hymns the Throne of the Almighty, the Seat of Wisdom, and so by analogy she became the root to the power, or, as Dante wrote: 'The Blessed Virgin is nine, for she is the root of the Trinity.'

Concluding the interview, the Dean said:

Thus, Master Scarlet, we the Chapter of the cathedral of Our Lady at Chartres instruct you to embody these numbers into every aspect of the design, and to remember, as I am sure

you will, that every step in the design of a sacred building must
be itself a devotion. So, may the Lord be with you, and may
Our Lady inspire you.

It would seem that meaning was in many ways going to be more
important than function or looks. The Chapter's insistence on number
was not unusual, for, as Augustine had written almost a thousand years
before: 'God made the world in measure, number and weight: and
ignorance of number prevents us from understanding things that are
set down in the scripture in a figurative and mystical way.'

Some of the best minds had for centuries been trying to understand
these things. They mattered as much to them as scientific things
matter to us, and were given much the same attention. They raised the
study of number, and of other symbolic concepts, to a very high art
indeed. Though it might offend our prejudices, we must never forget
that the world beyond the senses was more real to them than what they
saw or touched. The actual world that forms the basis of our reality
was for them merely a reflection, and often a poor one at that, of the
more important spiritual world.

Since the cathedral was to be the most Divine thing on earth, as the
symbol—and therefore at one level as the reality itself—of Paradise, it
had to incorporate every possible attribute of that spiritual reality. In
our day we call the church the House of God, for his presence occupies
it. But the thirteenth century was less circumspect. They had the
audacity to believe they were constructing a slice of eter . . . and
the simplicity to trust that God's Essence would be m . . .
something they built from the materials found on t . . .
achieved this by setting into the design as many of . . .
numbers and symbols as possible, so that the di . . .
meaning tumble over one another, layer upon laye . . .
reels under the weight.

Christianity is a progressive religion in which . . .
state of original sin towards a greater understandin . . .
pilgrim accepts a hierarchy of ideas when he com . . .
like the west being more mundane, from whic . . .
towards the altar and the rising sun at the east. His plac . . .
and he prays towards the choir. The root of our word 'nave' is the same
as navy, with its overtones of the ark, and of protection from the
boundless fears of the deep. The nave was reserved for the people, and

on the other side of the crossing the choir was preserved for the clergy. Within that lay the altar, and beyond that the invisible eastern doors that led to Paradise. Like the Heavenly Jerusalem, the church had twelve gates facing the four directions, and though the eastern ones were real, they were not of this world and therefore not visible. This axis represents man's process in comprehending the divine, and could therefore be called the axis of Understanding.

In the middle of the nave a huge pattern has been inscribed into the floor. It is the largest decorative item in the cathedral, and its purpose and obvious importance has mystified nearly all those who see it. This is the labyrinth. Its design is canonic, in that there are many examples in mediaeval churches, and that nearly all of those that date from this time follow exactly the same pattern. There are eleven rings, containing a path that leads by a circuitous but singular route to the middle. It is not a maze, but a way leading to the six-petalled rose at the centre. The arrangement is always the same: you enter on the left

51 The labyrinth, symbol of man's way to God here on earth.

and proceed directly to the fifth circle, then to the sixth, followed by all the inner rings and so on, to the centre. It must have had an important religious significance, otherwise why install it? Why make them so large? And why always use the same design? As with the masters, the documents are silent.

At one time there was a brass plaque at the centre. The three figures engraved on it, weird as they seem for a Christian church, tell us much about the meaning of this pattern. Two of the figures were the pagan mythological heroes Theseus and the Minotaur, and the third was Ariadne who supplied the string her lover used to find his way home. Theseus voluntarily searches for and finally destroys the devil, be it his original sin or his own inner passions, but having done so would have been lost in the darkness but for the guidance given him by his Virgin Lady. A nice Christian parable, and notice that even in the original myth Theseus, though betrothed to Ariadne, does not marry her, but leaves her behind so she remains a maid. For these reasons it is believed that the labyrinth portrays man's path to God, not after death, but now, while here on earth.

Later on I shall return to this important device, but first we must follow the path of the pilgrim into the building. He leaves the world of men, and enters through the doors of the Royal Portal on which are carved the basic truths of Christianity: that Christ was born and after death was physically resurrected. This is the proof of his Godhead. The entire superstructure of church theology and law rests on these truths, and they verify Mary's position as the Mother of God, and of Chartres as her especial home.

The doors fit between the two western towers. Two is the number of duality, of the first division of the Creation between the things of the spirit and the things of the world, between Essence and Substance. The towers are four-sided, which is 2 squared, and which in nearly all cultures represents the world of matter. Thus the pilgrim enters the cathedral from the end which symbolises the mundane from which he has come, and through doors whose truth he must accept if the rest is to be meaningful.

He then proceeds through the nave as ark, and over the labyrinth as the exemplification of his journey, towards the east. At the apse, the essential design consists of three large circular chapels. Three is the number of the spirit, again an almost universally accepted idea, and the circle, being the perfect figure without beginning or end, is God

52 The labyrinth. This is not a maze but a single way.

PUTTING SIGNIFICANCE INTO FORM · 87

himself. The pilgrim thus moves from the duality of existence towards the Trinity and the Spirit.

Just as the pilgrim moves towards Christ in and over the labyrinth, so at the altar Christ comes to him in the Eucharist. The contrariness of all things is implicit in every part of the cathedral. The opposites are posed clearly, appropriately balanced and reconciled. The building is a statement of the inner truths of life, with the contradictions separated and then placed in an orderly way against one another. The final statement is so integrated that what may have appeared to be confusion may be seen to stem from divine intelligence.

54 Two and three, squares and circles, in the plan all exemplify the pilgrims' way as progress.

The crossing lies at the exact centre of the design. Just as the square is the symbol of man's external setting, including the earth and, by extension, the walls of the city that give him security, so the cross is that of his internal state. Every place on earth can be located from the four cardinal points, and people who are unhappy often say they are 'disoriented'. The crossing represents the calm position of rest around which everything has been properly arranged. To the west is man's world with his path on earth, to the east is God's church with its power to bring him to the spirit.

In the other direction, passing at right angles to what I have called the axis of Understanding, lies another. I call this the axis of Knowledge. The clergy at Chartres adhered to the Platonic or Gnostic tradition, which taught that only through knowledge could God be successfully reached. They believed that study was as important as faith, for without philosophy we would be led astray and miss the true path. Hence knowledge and understanding went hand in hand, and though the former could achieve nothing without the latter, philosophy gave the pilgrim the same stability on his way as the well-cut feathers gave to the arrow. Hence the cross axis and the transepts which embodied it helped to centre the cathedral and to make it secure. These ideas are reinforced in the transept sculpture, which depicts the teachings of the Old Testament on the north and the New on the south.

The north is on the left-hand side of the building, looking from the west, and the south is on the pilgrim's right. The sculpture of the Old Testament and of things from the past are placed on the left, while the New Testament and the new covenant it embodied are all on the right. The left is universally considered the less beneficial aspect than the right. We can see this in the meanings we give words chosen from other languages. A person may be *gauche*, but in law there are *droits*, and from the Latin some people may be sinister but others are dextrous. Religious processions, like clocks, pass over the left-hand side before the right, and the principal guest sits on the host's right hand.

In the northern hemisphere these ideas are reinforced by the passage of the sun across the sky. It throws its full heat upon us from the south, while the cold Arctic winds blow down from the north. The setting sun, which in dying is less beneficial than the dawn rising behind the choir, illuminates the more mundane end of the cathedral. This concordance between spiritual ideas, the movement of the heavens and the seasons, and our inbred feelings for left and right is very exciting. John Harvey has translated the work of a clerkly poet from Lincoln, writing around this time about his own cathedral, that:

> the twin windows which display a circular splendour are the two
> eyes of the church: rightly the greater is the bishop, the lesser
> the Dean. From the north is the devil, to the south the Holy
> Ghost; towards these the two eyes look. For the bishop faces
> south that he may receive the one; the Dean north, that he may
> avoid the other; one looks to be saved, the other lest he perish.
>
> (1972, p. 238)

Before we see how Scarlet incorporated all these things into the plan, we must look at the difficult problems of accommodation during construction. Somehow the master had to provide a number of entrances into the crypt where they would not interfere with his yards and workshops, and to keep part of the main floor-level free for the clergy while he was working on the rest. The solution was an ingenious one, and was to have quite a big effect on the course of the works.

He saw that the old choir, as one of the brothers had said, could be repaired and used, at least for a few years. The slope of the land made this easier, for, as it was falling away towards the east, the walls around the crypt would be higher and would take longer to bring up to the choir floor level than those alongside the nave. He calculated that if he worked harder on the western end than the eastern he could probably delay the final demolition of Fulbert's damaged apse until the nave walls reached the level of the sills and could be roofed. Then the clergy could move out of the old apse into the new nave without the building work having to be stopped at either end. In this way he could work on the whole building, for even today a builder is shy of doing work in two stages when it can be done in one, if only because the setting out is more difficult, and the longer he spends on footings the more disturbed and untidy the site is going to be.

In fact it did not happen quite as neatly as this, for not all the contractors worked as fast on the nave as they might have done, while they all proceeded equally steadily with the demolition. The vaults over the old apse would have been mass concrete, and were not easy to pull down. A large ramp was constructed on the north side of the second chapel, and the débris was wheeled down this and dumped in what is now the Bishop's garden. Some day we may discover mouldings and capitals from the old building when we dig there, though I think that most of Fulbert's masonry ended up in the foundations, being just tipped into them as it was pulled out. Quick, simple and cheap.

For a few years this ramp prevented the masons from laying up the wall outside this part of the crypt, and by the time they could remove it the decision had been made to double the ambulatory in the apse. Rather than repeat the nasty arrangement found in the other chapels where the buttresses sat over the windows of the crypt, the master just closed them off so that two of the windows into the lower chapel are blank. This shows how much the master hated the idea of supporting structure over void, for he would rather cut out all the light to the crypt than do it.

Having decided to construct both ends of the building at the one time, and to preserve some part of the upper church for worship,

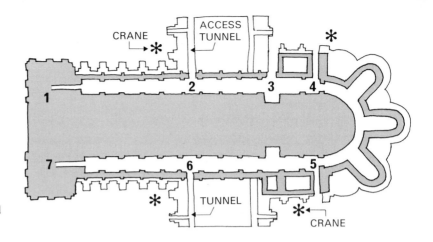

55 Openings 3, 4 and 5 into the crypt were closed during the major part of the rebuilding. 1 and 7 were accessible through the towers and the Royal Portal, and 2 and 6 through the new tunnels.

Scarlet had to find a way to connect it to the crypt. His solution is neat, and not to be found in other buildings. There were already seven doors into the crypt. The three eastern ones were too close to where he was going to build his big cranes, so he decided to close them off for the time being. The western ones could remain open as long as the narthex joined the western doors to the crypt entries inside the towers. But as these two would not be enough, he decided to keep the two middle ones open as well.

They were under the transepts, so tunnels were built as quickly as possible leading beyond the boundaries of the workshops, and off the side he placed narrow entries into the sides of the tunnels passing through the end buttresses, and which would be opened as soon as the end of the tunnel was blocked off by the porch stairs. Thus the pilgrims would be able to enter the crypt at four points, and as soon as the upstairs transept doors were opened, which was to be less than ten years after the fire, they could process out of the crypt through the tunnels and up the stairs into the body of the church. The timing of the tunnels and the movements they engendered suit the opening of the nave under a temporary roof in 1200, and of the choir and some of the doors a few years later. It was an ingenious solution that solved the clergy's problems without interfering with the work on the site.

But this was a small matter compared with the designing of the building itself. It was an age of church building, and the basic ideas and forms would have been as much a part of Scarlet's everyday imaginings as an office building or a block of flats might be today. I am sure he played with ideas even when he had no plans to do, as we find in the sketchbooks by his contemporary Villard de Honnecourt. The basic shape of the cathedral was otherwise established by the clergy in their brief, and by the remains of Fulbert's crypt. This form with the twin squares at the west and the triple circles at the east would have sat over the crypt with little difficulty, and the two axes, of Understanding and of Knowledge, would have readily located the crossing.

The diamonds shown in Fig. 56 would have been the next decision, as the first geometric step in giving order to the plan. Three equal diamonds set point to point in a row were symbolic of the Trinity, but this church had a different dedication. Eusebius describes the Virgin being flanked by her two humble bodyguards, and this may have been the origin of the hierarchic figure Scarlet chose. The large central

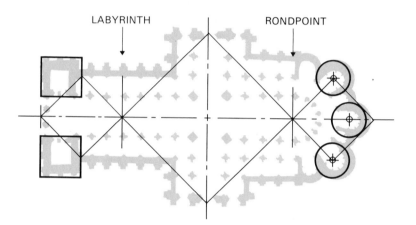

LABYRINTH   RONDPOINT

56 The basic design concept for the cathedral.

diamond was set round the crossing, and the two smaller ones encompass the towers at one end and the three chapels at the other. The nodal points are the centre of the rondpoint in the east and the labyrinth at the west. The importance of the labyrinth may be gauged by the crucial position it occupies in the first geometry. The centres of the two smaller diamonds passed through the side chapels in the east, and along the inside face of the towers at the west. The eastern sides framed the central chapel, and in the west the point precisely located the outside of the Royal Portal. The lateral points of the large diamond located the transept buttresses. Thus in one figure Scarlet has located the essential forms of the cathedral.

In every design process there is an awful step that many people, even experienced architects, have difficulty with. It is when the first design, roughed out with a 4B pencil in small sketches, has to be transformed into a scaled drawing. It is the moment of reality when the dreams are put aside and the truths of construction take over. It is often a cathartic moment, and in architecture it always involves one momentous step: the use of measure. Thinking of Augustine, it may have had religious significance too, for this is the point when number could be written into the design, and with number all the meanings it implies.

The lengths used to set out these diamonds were 241 feet, between the labyrinth and the rondpoint, and 354 feet, between the centres of the two flanking diamonds. The foot is not ours, but the Roman foot that Scarlet used every time he appeared on the site. These numbers are rather curious, for they are not immediately significant. Twenty-four times 10 would be much more obvious as twice the twelve apostles, or the tribes of Israel, etc., and similarly with thirty-six times 10. But 354? We will have to follow his whole design process through to the end before being able to answer this one.

Once Scarlet had determined the exterior envelope, he turned his attention to the interior. It is one of the curiosities of mediaeval architecture that few crossings are square in plan, and that the bays adjoining the crossing are slightly larger than the other bays down the nave or transepts. These puzzling arrangements can be seen in nearly every building of this period, and have been explained as being visual adjustments to maintain a balance between the first bays of the nave and the larger space of the crossing. At Chartres these bays are less than 10 cm wider than the others, and in any case mediaeval architecture is not in any way like the Greek: visual adjustments are not consistent with their stress on geometry, and it is to geometry that we must look for the answer.

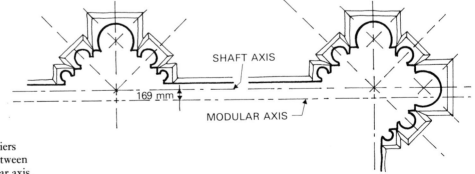

57 Wall and corner piers showing difference between Shaft axis and Modular axis.

Compare one of the typical wall shafts with the one at the corner of the transept. You can see that there are two axes running through the wall. One I have called the Modular or M axis, and it passes through the centre of the footings underneath. The other is the Shaft or S axis and on the right it passes through the shaft on the corner. The two axes are only 169 mm apart, and the master could have made them coincide by modifying the design of the corner. So why didn't he? The answer to this will give the clue to understanding the geometry for the interior.

The span between the Modular axes measures 112 feet, and was subdivided to form the simple 2:4:2 rhythm (Fig. 58) which is not only pleasing, but is simple to set out and was extended each way by one unit to locate the buttresses. This outer point lies on the diagonals from the corners of the buttresses, and is called the epicentre. If the master is designing around it, the axial centre remains constant even

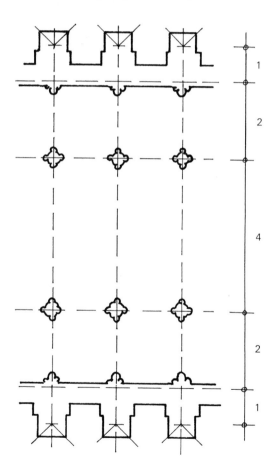

58 Three typical nave bays showing 1:2:4:2:1 ratios between the Modular axes.

when the buttress is reduced in size, as is usual in the upper parts. Not every master worked to this epicentre, but the majority did.

Through this series Scarlet linked the axes of the piers and the walls, which take the loads from the vaults, to the buttress epicentres that stabilise them.

But the origin of the Shaft axis is quite different. Where the M axes were positioned by using a module of so many feet, the S axes were derived geometrically. Their source is the hexagon, known as the perfect geometric figure, for any radius that is used to form the circle will make the sides of the hexagon, as any schoolgirl knows. Also 6 has an importance as twice the Trinity, and as one of the Perfect numbers which so fascinated mediaeval mathematicians. These are those numbers whose factors will add up to the number itself. The factors of 6 are 1, 2 and 3, which will sum to 6. The next number in the series is 28, and after that 496. There is only one of them before ten, one between that and a hundred, and only one more between a hundred and a thousand. Also, a fact the middle ages did not know, there is only one between a thousand and ten thousand. They also have other curious mathematical qualities that need not concern us, but which intrigued them so much that the length of the major church of the Cluniac monastic order was deliberately designed as the sum of the first three Perfect numbers.

To establish the S axes Scarlet set out two hexagons. He first drew a circle 112 feet in diameter, which was the dimension used in the Modular series, and inside that he drew a hexagon. This located the wall and pier axes running east–west. In the same direction it positioned the first pair of piers flanking the crossing, marked N in Fig. 59. The master then drew a second circle, shown in the lower half of the drawing, with a diameter of 96 feet. Round that he drew another hexagon, but this time outside the circle rather than inside it. It lay within the first hexagon and located the S axes and, along the north–south axis, the first piers in the transepts, marked T.

The crossing itself was formed from half of each of these dimensions so that it formed a rectangle of 56 by 48 feet. They are in the proportion 7:6. Besides the meanings that might be given to these numbers, the 6 lies in the direction of the long axis of the building and the 7 in the other. The long axis of Understanding is Christ's, while the cross axis of Knowledge is Mary's, for Christ said: 'I am the Way', while Mary was the patron of all philosophy. The long axis should

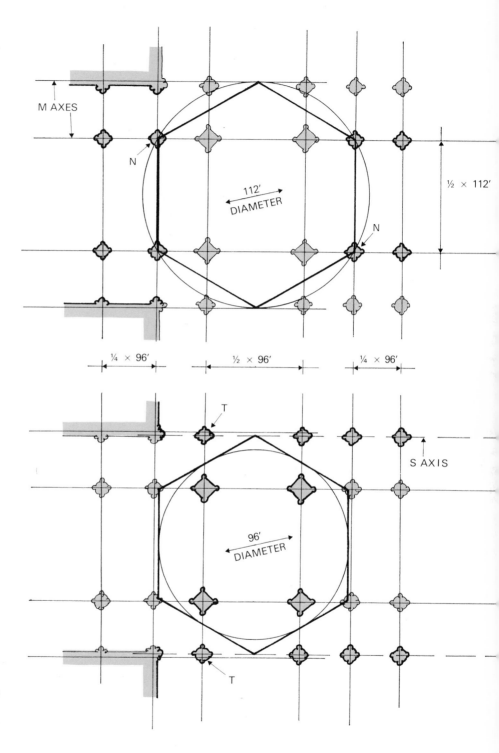

M AXES

N

112′
DIAMETER

½ × 112′

¼ × 96′   ½ × 96′   ¼ × 96′

N

T

S AXIS

96′
DIAMETER

T

59 In these two plans of the crossing the hexagon in the upper one determines the M axes and the flanking columns on the choir and nave sides. In the lower drawing the smaller hexagon locates the S axes and the piers on the transept sides.

contain the Perfect number in its ratio, just as Christ is the Perfect Man, while the transept axis should contain 7, for philosophy was her special prerogative as patron of the seven Liberal Arts.

Thus the two hexagons derived from only two lengths were used by Scarlet to position the crossing, the piers that surround it, and the two M and S axes within the walls. To achieve so much from so little was one of the aims of mediaeval geometry, and brings us to another. Scarlet has combined two contrary modes: modules in the $1:2:4:2:1$ series and in the $7:6$ crossing, and irrationals in the $\sqrt{3}$ found in the hexagon. The two axes, the Modular and the Shaft, reflect the two systems. As there is no way that modular and geometric figures can be exactly reconciled, the masters had to accept this gap. Indeed, they seem to have welcomed it, for they deliberately chose to use both, and then accepted the struggle needed to bring them together.

It is as if they deliberately posed numbers against geometry so that they could put themselves to the labour of resolving the unresolvable. This troublesome attitude was not rare, but quite typical of the middle ages. They saw the world in polarities. Ambivalence was inherent in the first act of Creation. To every black there was a white, to every aspect could be found its antithesis. It was as fundamental to the universe as the world itself, and dominated all manifest reality like the square twin spires that flank each side of the western doors. In philosophy as in architecture they strove to reach beyond the poles to that calm centre where all is one. The basic endeavour of geometricians was the same as that of the Schoolmen: to reconcile the irreconcilable, and this they 'perfected into a fine art that determined the form of academic instruction, the ritual of the public *disputationes de quodlibet* and above all the process of argumentation in the Scholastic writings themselves. Every topic had to be formulated' in a particular way, writes Panofsky (1956, pp. 67–8). 'Needless to say, this principle was bound to form a mental habit no less decisive and all-embracing than that of unconditional clarification', which epitomises the modern scientific view.

This habit was reflected in geometry no less than in philosophy. We tend today to ride over the differences so as to discover the common laws that lie within them all. We reduce the multiplicity of life to its basic common factors. The middle ages abhorred sameness and uniformity. They gloried in multiplicity as part of the Divine order, for simplicity denies the first principle of manifestation, that of duality.

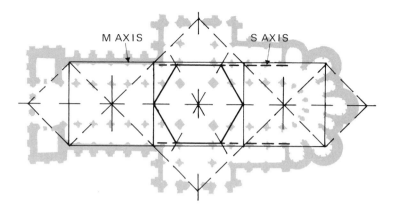

60 The S axis hexagon fits inside the diamonds.

Hence we should not be surprised when we find more than one geometric system inhabiting the one place, each flowing over the other, while being locked together at a few essential points like the labyrinth and the altar, which thereby express the most sacred and meaningful locations in the building.

Returning to the plan for Chartres, we can see that for a building of this importance there would have to be a number of geometric systems. Externally there is the one with the three diamonds, and internally there are the two hexagons and the M and S axes they engendered. But they could not be left alone, unconnected. They had to be reconciled, and the steps taken to do that were not too difficult, in retrospect. The master worked both ways, from each figure in turn to the other. Within the diamonds he formed the two squares shown in Fig. 60 centred on the labyrinth and on the rondpoint, and the hexagon forming the Shaft axis could then be fitted snugly between them.

Then he worked outwards from the hexagon that formed the M axes. To it he added six bays, three on either side of the centre (Fig. 61). The span of each was that of the crossing, or half the 112-foot circle that had formed this hexagon, while the distance the other way was half the crossing, or one-quarter of the circle that had formed the Shaft hexagon. This composite figure, of three-bays-plus-hexagon-plus-three-bays, fitted precisely within the large diamond, meeting it at the centres of the labyrinth and the rondpoint. So we now have one simple and complete arrangement for the cathedral, totally integrated yet essentially irreconcilable, which I have called the Creation Figure. I could go on and show how from this the walls, the piers, the shafts which run up them, the chapels and indeed every last detail of the plan

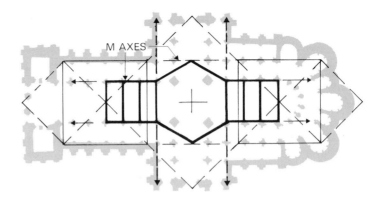

M AXES

61 The M axis hexagon also fits inside the diamonds.

was evolved from this first figure. Nothing in the plan is irrelevant or accidental. The proof for this geometry, if we need one, lies in the holistic consistency between it and every part of the building.

I shall give one example only, as it has to do with meanings. The typical bay now has a proportion that stems from the crossing, and is half of it at $7:3$. The span, being 7, was divided into ninths, and the bay, being 3, was divided into fifths, producing fractions each time. Then diamonds were formed from the ninths and squares from the fifths. The two were laid over one another to produce a sort of octagon, and the huge piers with the central drum and four engaged shafts were derived from it. The octagon then remained as the footing underneath the pier, and the widths of the ninths and fifths were extended to the

62 Base of one of the piers in the nave showing the 'octagonal' footing course which here projects out of the floor.

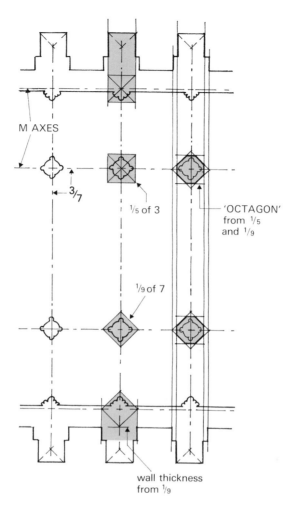

M AXES

3/7

1/5 of 3

'OCTAGON'
from 1/5
and 1/9

1/9 of 7

wall thickness
from 1/9

63 Typical nave piers, showing successive divisions which produced the 'octagon' footing under the piers, which in their turn derived from the octagon.

outside, as you can see in Fig. 63, to locate the sides of the buttresses.

Besides the nice unity this gave to the interior and to its external supports, and the suitable size and shape the octagon gave him for the piers, there were meanings in his choice of numbers. For the long axis was divided into fifths, and 5 is the number of Christ as the man born (= 4) and consecrated (= 1). It is the 4 of materiality plus the 1 of the All. While 9, the subdivisor of the cross axis, is Mary's second number. The foundations of the building are therefore as dependent on Mother and Child as are the original proportions, and the sculptures that show the child Jesus enthroned on the lap of Mary. Thus down the length of the cathedral along the Christ axis we find the numbers 3, 5 and 6, while along the other are both of Mary's, 7 and 9.

When the clergy instructed Scarlet to use the two Mary numbers of 7 and 9 in the plan for the building they were not joking. Neither was he. Examine Fig. 64 and see for yourself. There are nine bays in the nave from the crossing to the Royal Portal, and seven within the nave from the two large piers just east of the towers. There are seven bays across the transepts, and nine from the labyrinth to the rondpoint. In the apse there are seven chapels, and there would have been nine with those in the sanctuary. The cathedral had been planned for nine towers, there are nine doorways, and there are altogether sixty-three rectangles forming the aisles and naves, which is seven times nine.

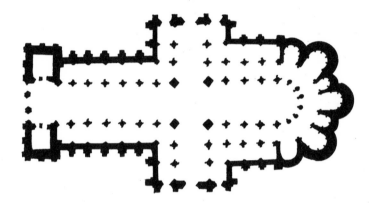

64 The original plan for the cathedral as prepared by master Scarlet in 1194.

'God made the world in measure, number and weight'—they took Augustine seriously. Yet to our eyes one of the results is unfortunate. At the western end of the nave the three bays between the labyrinth and the towers were smaller than the others, the last one being positively squashed. It was thought at one time that they had intended to pull down the western towers with the rest of the burnt-out building and to erect a new one, but that having started to set out the nave, they changed their mind and decided to leave it. As George Henderson so delightfully puts it, 'the architect's manoeuvres in the last two western bays are nothing so much as the screeching of brakes. He ran up against an obstacle, where he had hoped to have a clear run home.' (1968, p. 95)

The facts do not support this engaging theory, for, as we all know, truth is indeed stranger than fiction. The facts are that the whole of the nave, including these three uncomely bays, were set out and built in one piece. In no other part of the building is the coursing so uniform, the bases all from the same templet, and the walling and superstructure so similar. There are no joints here, and we must accept that Scarlet *intended* to do this. The reason seems to lie in geometry and number. The building had to be set out from a coherent and unified geometric system, and this was more important than appearance. There was no escaping this essential prerequisite. Equally the clergy had insisted that the Virgin's own special numbers be used throughout. If Scarlet could have made the nave eight bays long with only six from the crossing to the towers, he need not have squeezed up the end, nor need he have cut into the structure of the towers by over a metre in some places to get the last bay in. It was a shoehorn operation, but not because the clergy had changed their minds.

The clergy's ideas on number and the master's on geometry had to be squeezed within the solid boundaries formed by the remains of the old building. Their choices, as the results show, prove beyond any doubt that geometry was the most powerful factor in the design, and that it, rather than concepts of beauty, determined the arrangement. Aesthetics is a nineteenth-century gloss on renaissance thinking, and would seem to have little place in the mediaeval panorama.

Having designed the building, Scarlet deliberately bent the axes. There was no need to do this, for he had a relatively simple situation to deal with. It could not have been a mistake, for the setting out along the walls of the nave is so accurate there is less than an inch of error in any of the buttresses. Yet at the rondpoint the axis has been moved to the south by a foot, exactly one of Scarlet's Roman feet. There are some twists in the other axes, too, forming a coherent and orderly system of sways and bends that belie the possibility of randomness, and therefore of error.

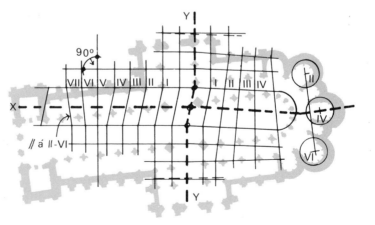

65 At the piers of the rondpoint the east–west axis was offset one Roman foot to the south and the cross axes were twisted to suit the existing misalignments of the west front and the eastern chapels of the crypt.

Bent axes are quite common in Christian churches, and have in the past been put down to mistakes or to difficulties with property boundaries or the like. If these axes were twisted in all directions I would agree with these theories, but they are not, as you can see if you observe them. How many are there that bend to the north? To my knowledge there are scarcely any. Draw a straight line from the centres of the end walls of any bent mediaeval building and the axes *will nearly always lie to the south of it.* Can this be anything but a purposeful device?

Architecturally, bending the axis is an attempt to avoid symmetry, for it adds the same sort of imbalance that we find in natural things. Examine each side of your face, and you will see slight differences. A doll may be beautiful, but its flawless perfection is lifeless whether she be living or not. The artist knows this, and the masters could have known too, but did the clergy? None of the documents mentions bends in buildings, but neither do they mention labyrinths. The only contemporary writings I know of are from India, and though I am not suggesting any connection between them, it does at least suggest a way of looking at the problem.

Indian temples are symmetrical boxes in plan in which there is no way to bend the axis. But the Vastu-Shastras instruct the architect to avoid the 'vulnerable spots' by moving the lingam a few barleycorns to the north of the axis. Notice that their altar was moved to the north, which achieves the same effect as moving the axis itself to the south and leaving the altar where it is. Most sophisticated religions believe that there is a discrepancy between the ideal and the actual. No matter how small it may be, there will always be this tiny residue from which comes all the diversity within a species. The Indians believed that this residue opens a window into the Infinite.

In this case I do not believe that the clergy had anything to do with the bend. Important as this idea was theologically, it seems that the vital decision was Scarlet's alone. I say this because his successor Bronze straightened this axis. He found it bent, and on arrival reduced the depth of the southern buttresses by 470 mm, and altered all the cross axes where he could to bring them into true. If the clergy had authorised the bent axis for its sacred significance, surely they would have told the second master to keep it that way. The fact that it was straightened shows otherwise. And interestingly the third and fifth masters tried to bend it again, the others adhering to the straight. Half for each idea, a proportion that is not inconsistent with the number of churches found today with bent axes.

This suggests some fascinating possibilities about the masters' traditions. They must have flowed through the ages independently of their patrons, and have evolved as concepts and theories within a culture of their own. Maybe there is something in the beliefs held by the Masonic lodges after all. Their traditions lasted until the end of the middle ages, as far as we can see at this moment, but died out with the coming of the professional architect in the sixteenth century.

If the masters evolved, and passed on exclusively among themselves, a tradition for expressing sacred ideas in stone, we would have to accept the presence of a parallel culture within a mediaeval society, running alongside but seldom mixing with the Establishment of clergy and nobility. Did they have connections with the Scholastic philosophers or the alchemists? Did the masters work out their own ideas independently of one another? The way some bent the axis and others did not—like the different ways in which the basic forms of the plan were combined in the churches, few of which follow the same arrangement—shows this may be so. Number and its meanings were probably the clergy's provenance, but geometry and length seem to have been the masters'. The number of bays remains unaltered no matter who is the master, but the geometry changes with each campaign. And it is here, in the lengths used for the first plan, that we find the most awesome example of the masters' sacral traditions.

We might call the four lengths mentioned earlier the shouts that launched the avalanche. For without the 112 foot and 96 foot circles, and the 241 foot and 354 foot diamonds, the geometry, and hence the building, could not have been started. The reasons for them are not easy to uncover. We have so little to go on. Many people believe that the masters and the clergy must have sought in one way or another to begin their designs with something that would symbolically relate the building to sacred concepts. Many theories have been propounded over the years, but sadly we do not have one unequivocal document that would confess to what they did. There are of course many contemporary books describing the symbolism of the parts of the church, not unlike the poem by the Lincoln monk quoted earlier, but there is nothing describing the initial act in the design.

Let us start with the proposition that the cathedral is God's home, in the real sense which raises it above the level of symbols. The cathedral is his earthly Jerusalem and must therefore contain as much of his Essence as man can devise. We have already seen how this could be done in the form of the building, in the numbers incorporated within it and the geometry of diamonds and hexagons. But there is another technique for expressing concepts in architecture, and it is also to do with number, though it is more sophisticated. It is called gematria. It was known long before Christ, and was brought into mediaeval Europe by both Christian and Hebrew scholars.

The technique was to translate important liturgic phrases into numbers by giving each letter of the alphabet a number, A being 1, B is 2, C 3, and so on. Then these numbers are substituted for the letters of the phrase and added together, to give one large figure for the whole expression. Thus the important Mary phrase, 'Sedes Sapientie', in which she is given the title of the Throne of Wisdom, would total 144 in the Latin alphabet used at the time. The fact that this number is twelve times 12, the number of the fulfilment of creation, and twice the number of Mary herself as 'Mater Dei', would tend to add to its original significance. Further, the digits in 144 add up to 9, which is one of the Virgin's numbers, while 'Virgine' sums to 9^2, being 81.

However dubious *we* may find such cryptograms, their creation and their mystic interpretation goes back to writers of exceptional reputation in classical and mediaeval times. The American scholar Conant, who spent his life investigating the ruined abbey at Cluny, wrote:

> The philosophers perceived that number, being perfectly abstract, can therefore be shared by all three worlds: physical, spiritual and mystical. Beautiful patterns of spiritual thought are elaborated by the adepts in symbolic numerical studies—patterns which give pure joy because they are entirely uncontaminated by mundane or temporal things. The philosophers considered that the beauty, order and stability of the universe depended on number. (1963, p. 13)

The real flavour for this fascinating play with numbers is still with us, and has been evocatively described by Herman Hesse in a futuristic novel inspired by numerology.

> These rules, the sign language and grammar of the game, constitute a kind of highly developed secret language drawing

upon several sciences and establishing interrelationships between the content and conclusions of nearly all scholarly disciplines. The Glass Bead Game is thus a mode of playing with the total concepts and values of our culture. All the insights, noble thoughts, and works of art that the human race has produced in its creative eras, all that subsequent periods of scholarly study have reduced to concepts and converted into intellectual property—on all this immense body of intellectual values the Glass Bead Game player plays like the organist on an organ, which is theoretically capable of reproducing the entire intellectual content of the universe. (1922, pp. 18–19)

Here in number and in the proper disposition of the shapes which go with it the men of older times attempted to represent no less than the entire spiritual content of the universe. Though little is documented for buildings, we know that these methods were used by poets and musicians. Using the notes of the sol–fa scale, composers would begin by arranging the melody from the vowels found in the text. 'Sedes Sapientie' would be noted as re–re for the two vowels of the first word and by fa–mi–re–mi–re for the second, creating a verbal–musical pun which could then be adapted in tempo to suit the mood and occasion. Then by cutting and expanding, by transposing and repeating this basic unit, the piece of music would be built up. So it is not surprising that musicians like Dufay were called 'mathematici'.

Experimenting with this technique I found that the two lengths used to form the diamonds in the Creation Figure could have come from phrases of unique relevance to the cathedral of Chartres.

The cathedral is dedicated to the Virgin, but that can be said of many churches. Chartres is the only one to be specifically dedicated to her bodily Assumption. It was an extremely popular belief at the time, even though it was not canonic law, and was not to become so until the 1950s. The belief that she sat on the right hand of God gave Chartres most of her kudos. So, maybe it is not so surprising to find that the 241 feet forming the central diamond is the sum of the phrase 'Beata Virgo Maria Assumpta'. It in fact sums to 240, but in gematria 1, representing the Godhead, may be added to or subtracted from any number. The Assumed Blessed Virgin Mary is the dedication of the cathedral, and how right that it should inaugurate both the axes through the crossing and the diamond that sits astride it.

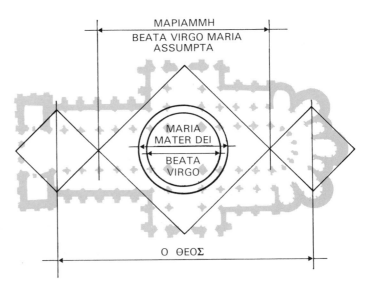

MAPIAMMH
BEATA VIRGO MARIA
ASSUMPTA

MARIA
MATER DEI

BEATA
VIRGO

Ο ΘΕΟΣ

66 Phrases used to set out the Creation Figure.

There are two ways of counting in gematria. The straightforward series of numbers from 1 to 22 applied to the Latin alphabet, known as the Lesser Canon, and another when the letters after the tenth are numbered 20, 30, and so on up to 100, and the remainder in hundreds. This latter is known as the Greater, or Greek, Canon. Greek numbers had been written as letters from the sixth century before Christ. It was an adaptation of an even earlier system employed by the people of the Euphrates basin, and brought westwards by the Israelites after their captivity in Babylon. In the Greater Canon the first ten letters were counted in the same way as the Lesser, but thereafter the counting proceeded in tens, and then in hundreds. In the Greater Canon, 240 spells 'MAPIAMMH', while the second long dimension of 354 feet lying down the axis of the Understanding is the sum of the important phrase 'Ο ΘΕΟΣ'. Thus both Mother and Son have been enshrined down the length of the cathedral. Christ down the long axis lies supported on the Virgin's diamond which, as was sung in the hymns, signified she was 'the Throne of the Almighty'.

As if this was not enough, the hexagons themselves come from two other important phrases. Returning to the Lesser Canon, the larger circle spells 'Maria Mater Dei', while the smaller one gives us 'Beata Virgo'.

The phrases are long, the numbers they produce are large, and the possible options are few indeed. Yet here we have all four first lengths perfectly adumbrated in number. Even lacking the textual evidence, it is more than possible that this is how Scarlet created the first plan and brought theology into it. The masters have left no descriptions of how they designed or laid out their buildings, the few surviving clerical texts are silent on this subject. So I am doubtful about the church's role in this aspect of the master's work, for surely if the clergy had normally given the masters the opening phrase for the work we would somewhere over five centuries have found some reference to this use of

67 The unbroken walls which enclose the transepts reflect the meanings inherent in the geometric figure that positioned them.

gematria. We do have texts that show they knew the code, and they used it on small items. But we have no written evidence from churchmen that they applied it to long sacred phrases, or that they instructed their architects to implant them into architecture. It therefore seems to be the joy of the master, again suggesting there may have been a tradition within a tradition.

Having set out the major form of the building, Scarlet proceeded to write a number of other ideas into it. I shall describe two only. He placed a large hexagon within the plan, this time with its points on the labyrinth and the centre of the rondpoint. It was therefore contained within the circle that also enclosed the large central diamond. The sides positioned the inside faces of the end walls of the transepts.

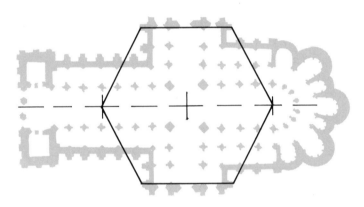

68 The large hexagon which locates the transept walls.

Just as the crossing at the centre of the cathedral came from two hexagons, so a third determined the most important spacial barriers within it. Stand within the crossing and note how the real form of the enclosure flows from the labyrinth to the rondpoint down the axis of Understanding and, like a river, is enclosed by solid embankments at the ends of the transepts. The invisible powers concentrated at the former are poised against the material solidity of the latter. Spirit and matter have been succinctly separated and thereby defined, spirit through the corners of the hexagon and matter along its sides. Abbot Suger of St Denis may have produced the specification of this when he wrote in the 1140s that 'the dull mind rises to the Truth through the material'. Is this why the material walls of the transepts are the only blank ones in the cathedral, without any windows from the floor to the triforium?

For the second set of ideas Scarlet incorporated into the plan he used his larger second foot unit of 353 mm. There are exactly $365\frac{1}{4}$ of them from the inside of the western front to the inside of the axial chapel—the number of days in the year. Coincidence, you will say. Then let's see. The most important astronomical calculations undertaken in the middle ages were to compute accurately the dates for Easter. Though dependent on the moon, the dates still had to keep in step with the cycle of the solar year. This they did through a simple formula, where for two years running they fixed Easter from the short year of thirteen lunations, followed by one long or embolismic year of 384 days which, with suitable adjustments, brings the Easter cycle back into phase with the sun.

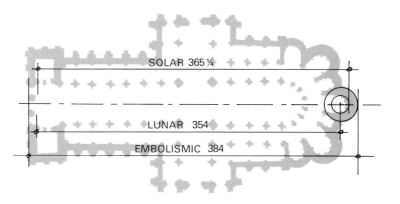

SOLAR 365 ¼

LUNAR 354

EMBOLISMIC 384

69 The Easter dating set into the cathedral.

The length of the lunar year is 354 days, and there are 354 of Scarlet's longer feet from the inside of the western front to the centre of the axial chapel. And, wait for it, there are 384 feet from the outside of the west front to the outside face of the chapel. All three of the numbers needed for calculating the cycle of Easter are included in the plan. Who said that something becomes magical when it accumulates many meanings? Is it any wonder that we still approach this cathedral with awe, when the architect who designed it pursued his work with such extraordinary sensitivity.

If the master was responsible for all these things, what sort of man was he? What was his training, especially in religious matters? Examining the work of the nine masters at Chartres, it would seem that only two of them show this intense aptitude for significance. The best among the others have a profound sense for architectural and

70 The colonnette-encrusted buttresses around the south transept that separates the nave from the choir.

geometric analysis, with all the permutations this could involve, but none of them shows evidence of having sought such spiritual expression. It may be that the eminence of Chartres stems from the first plan having been created by such a man, who was not only a great architect but also a cunning geometrician and a profound philosopher. Scarlet's greatness of soul and the appropriateness of his knowledge mark him as a most exceptional man. Though we find his mark on the cathedral only five times, it is substantially his monument. We know the great artist by his works; in Chartres, Scarlet created the greatest cathedral in Christendom.

7
THE ARCHITECT

SCARLET WAS THE first contractor and began the lowest courses which established the shape of the cathedral. We know that Scarlet left the site after less than a year to be replaced by Bronze, and we also know there was a permanent staff of clergy to supervise the builders and to provide them with funds. But was there an architect as well, either as a member of this committee, or as an independent professional employed by them for the term of the works?

Could Chartres have been organised like the Seagram building in New York? The nominated architect was Mies van der Rohe, but being retired and not interested in the arduous task of co-ordinating such a complex structure, he chose another architect with his own office to do the work for him. Philip Johnson was in law the architect, and he chose the builder and supervised the work. Yet there is not one design decision that did not have Mies's authority. This is not to say that some of the ideas were not Johnson's, for he contributed the lighting system, many details and accessories like doors and taps. How could we disentangle the masters on a job like this?

The role of the architect has been defined many times from Vitruvius onwards. Common to all of these definitions is his total responsibility for the design and its structural stability. We could not imagine an architect who left the designing of the building to others, for then he would be neglecting his role as the artist, nor could we imagine one who let the builder alter the structure as he thought fit. Remove either of these functions and we no longer have the architect, but someone else. Indeed, they influence one another, for if the shape of the buttress or pier is altered for structural reasons then so is the design, for the new shape will affect the appearance.

I am quite prepared to accept that the architect may have left the design of the minor items to the men on the job. The shape of the cornices, the small windows and doors and so on could all have been amended from time to time without changing the overall authority. As these are on the whole just the items I have used to distinguish one contractor from another, they do not affect the argument. Even small structural things could have been altered by the builders and as long as their changes did not modify the design the architect could have permitted them. For example, in the rooms under the towers at the level of the triforium the ribs are supported on pilasters. In some cases the pilasters are set true to the wall and in others they project at 45°, while in some there are no pilasters at all, as the ribs rest on corbels, or even on no corbels at all.

But what of the big changes in the cathedral, such as Bronze's straightening of the axis? And the other momentous alterations that followed, when he cut half a metre off the buttress on the southern side of the apse and realigned many of the interior piers? And, most important, his decision to increase the size of the crossing, which made him rearrange the spacing in the choir between the crossing and the rondpoint?

Scarlet's crossing was in the ratio of 7:6. Bronze enlarged this space to $\sqrt{5}:2$, which is not as difficult as it looks, for this expression is simply the mathematical equivalent of drawing a double square to represent 2, and employing the diagonal for the $\sqrt{5}$. He had a good reason for making the crossing this way, for it is the first step in constructing his favourite ratio that he was to use throughout the building, the golden mean. Not only would it then be appropriately enshrined at the centre of the cathedral, but the crossing could be used at any stage to check the accuracy of the other dimensions stemming from it.

This meant he had to move the eastern walls of the transept outwards to match the movement in the crossing, and he actually brought these walls out of the ground with three of the end buttresses by the porches. But the eastern crossing piers were not started by Bronze, probably because the old apse was still in place. This was to be the task of his successor, Rose, who pulled out the interfering bays of the burnt-out church and poured the remaining crossing footings. He placed them to suit a different geometry altogether with a smaller crossing. He therefore moved the inside face of the eastern walls of the transepts westwards, making those walls a metre thicker than the ones on the opposite side.

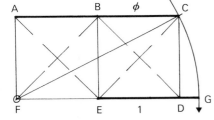

71 To construct the golden mean draw the double square ACDF. The diagonal FC being $\sqrt{5}$ is swung to FG. Then EG:AC = 1:φ.

72 The great piers of the
crossing.

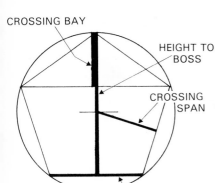

CROSSING BAY

HEIGHT TO BOSS

CROSSING SPAN

HEIGHT TO SPRINGING

73 The large pentagon from which Rose positioned all the elements within his parts of the building.

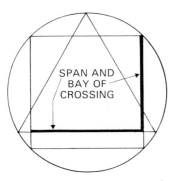

SPAN AND BAY OF CROSSING

74 The Alchemist's figure used by Olive to finalise the dimensions of the crossing.

Rose was the third master, and liked to use pentagons. He is the only one of the nine masters of Chartres who dared work with this difficult figure. He used the radius and one of the verticals of an enormous pentagon for the two dimensions of the crossing, as shown in Fig. 73. It would seem that they established these great dimensions in the building by setting out the geometry full size in a field near the town, and then transferred these accurate dimensions on rods or ropes to the site. I think Scarlet too would have had to set out the entire cathedral on a somewhat larger field before beginning to build it, for only in this way would he have ensured that the final building would coincide with all the relationships we find there.

I would have doubted this pentagonal figure had Rose not come back to the building in later years to establish the height of the capitals under the high vaults, and later the boss over the crossing. Both these decisions fitted so precisely into the same figure, with building errors of only a centimetre or so, that I had to credit him with the pentagon. Here is one master co-ordinating the entire interior of the building, as far as he was able. It is like a fugue running inside the work of others, where a single shape determined all the parts he had responsibility for. The idea is amazing, as indeed is the execution, for it is not at all easy to set out a pentagon, let alone build it to this sort of accuracy.

However, Rose's work on the lowest courses of the crossing piers stopped at floor-level on the eastern side. The actual plinths were laid by his successor Olive in 1197, and he made adjustments, too, by moving them a little over the footings. Not much, for there was no room for him to do more, but enough to change the geometry. Olive is a unitary master, interested in groupings of related components. Thus in his windows and doors he used sequences like $\sqrt{2}:\sqrt{3}:\sqrt{5}$ and $3:4:5$. In the crossing he combined together the square, the circle and the triangle into a single figure that looks just like one of the many illustrations in books of alchemy. It may have been his way of obtaining a mystic unity, for I have found him using the same sort of arrangements elsewhere in the building.

I think this resolves the question of the client's involvement in the concepts underlying the design of the cathedral. What can be seen and counted from the ground, like the general format of the plan and the number of bays and storeys, would certainly come under his scrutiny. But the variations in measurement from campaign to campaign show indubitably that the supervisor never carried a rule with him, and never asked questions about the geometry. These matters were left to the master mason. They were part of the craft that enabled him to execute the work, while the plan, the form and number of bays was, like the iconography, left to the clergy. They each had their respective spheres of expertise, and seemed on the whole to stay within them.

However, this resolves nothing about the architect. Where is he among all these changes to the crossing and the axes? None is structural, for the same-sized piers were being used at each stage, but they are aesthetic, for they affect the look of the interior. And, more important, they completely negated all the subtleties of the original plan and its amazing geometry. If the architect was in command over these years, how did he feel about his carefully considered arrangement as it was pushed about? He had squeezed the western bays of the nave so as to preserve the purity of the geometry, yet he was powerless to prevent that geometry being dismantled by the first change of builders. Maybe during the first three years while the client was paying for the works himself he decided to save on architect's fees and have him down only for the preliminary planning. Once he was able to raise funds elsewhere, he may have brought him back again. But did he?

In 1197 Olive laid out the plinths under the walls of the southern transept. Because of all the changes that had occurred so far, few of the axes between the piers were straight. He wished to keep equal centres between the piers, so none of the aisles was square, nor were any of the bays across the space of the transept itself. One of his tricks was to align the outer face of the plinth underneath the wall shaft true to the centre of the pier opposite. It was a sort of sympathetic magic, as if by

75 The end bays in the south transept.

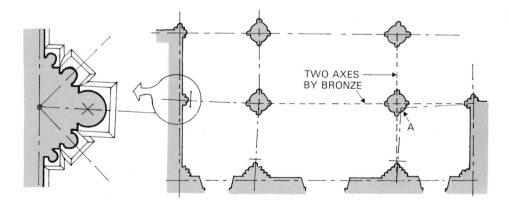

TWO AXES BY BRONZE

A

aligning the plinths, the shaft—and therefore the wall behind it—would be more capable of dealing with the loads coming on to it.

On the eastern side the wall shafts point to where the pier would have been if Olive had put it down, marked A. But the pier is not there. It has been shifted a few centimetres to one side by Bronze, and you can see why. Olive's crazy shifts in the axes were anathema to him, so he ran a string-line from the wall shaft to the already partly-constructed pier on the western side of the transept, and another string from the crossing to the southern wall, and simply placed the pier on their intersection.

These distinctions may seem small in the centimetres involved, like a storm in a teacup. But underneath they represent very important differences in the way the masters viewed the function of structure. The final judgment on a structure may be stated like this: Is it the most economic arrangement that will continue for an indefinite time to withstand the loads placed upon it? In a Gothic building the loads are lateral as well as vertical, and these buildings are much more likely to collapse from being pushed over than from the crushing of the stonework. So the direction in which these side thrusts are taken is of great importance. Such a vital alteration in the structure shows that there must have been a change in architects, and we can date that change between 1197 and 1198.

In chapter 2 I described how Scarlet had transformed Ruby's nave sills into walkways, and how Bronze had altered the single windows into double ones. Both these decisions could have been made by the one architect, in which case the sloping sill would have been the work of the 1198 appointee, and the next change in architects would have occurred when the drip was made into a cornice in 1200. So, did the new architect of 1198 last only two years?

In 1203 the buttresses were eliminated between the chapels of the apse. You can see in Fig. 76 that the buttress was to have been rectangular, but that above the cornice it has become no more than a shape to fill in the corner. In the next year the rectangular buttresses begun over the walkway to the western bay of the sanctuary were not repeated in the eastern bay, but were changed into 'T' shapes, and the geometry is quite different. And again in 1206 Ruby built the left-hand buttress over the southern porch, making it narrower, longer and differently aligned from the one Bronze had earlier built on the right.

Each of these changes in 1203, 1204 and 1206 involves different

76 The buttress between two of the chapels which supports one of the flyers round the apse. How many different schemes do you see?

77 The recesses called ostiums, each containing a statue, which complete the nave buttresses.

approaches to thrusts, different ways to calculate the length of the buttress from the span, and even different points within the wall and the buttress from which these lengths were calculated. If the one architect was on the job all the time, then he was changing his structural engineer almost every year: which would be the same as saying that he changed his builder. In which case it was the builder, not the architect, who looked after the structure.

Can we argue that the architect was solely a professional designer, concerned only with the larger issues, who left not only the details, but the geometry and the structure to his builders? If he was, then his concern for the design left a lot to be desired, as can be seen in the history of the crossing, and the meagre buttresses forced on the

78 The aedicules capping the buttresses of the choir.

sanctuary through the changes Bronze made to the axes.

Between 1207 and 1209 a series of modifications were made within the attic rooms that are purely structural, and would have had no effect on the appearance from the ground. But during the same years the number of columns within the openings of the triforium was increased from five to six, and the pitch of the roofs round the perimeter of the choir was raised from 8° to 50°. These two decisions profoundly altered the density of the interior and the external silhouette. So when both the structure and the design of the building seem to be changing year by year in spite of the architect, what can we say about him?

Let us still give him credit for maintaining some sort of unity over the design. It could not be much, for so many things were being altered. But surely we must still have someone overseeing the macro-decisions like the uniformity of the interior? Or must we? Compare Figs 77 and 78 with the colonnette-encrusted façade of the south front in Fig. 70. The south was begun by Ruby in 1211 when he placed the bottom courses of the buttresses on top of the triforium walkway. In the same year he was the proud winner of the competition for the clerestory windows, and had begun to lay them out in the nave. But in the very next campaign Cobalt laid the external plinths under the nave buttresses, and they were to be plain, without any colonnettes whatsoever. Now why would the colonnettes not be continued all round the building? Why single out the transept for special treatment? Buttresses in other buildings had been encased in them, so why not here?

In Fig. 77 see how the upper part of the buttress was finished with a recess or ostium containing a statue, and it is capped with a small roof. This was the work of Scarlet in 1215, in the same year as he began the flyers in the nave with their massive arches and spokes. In the very next year Ruby came back again, and instead of repeating the ostiums in the choir, he produced the scheme in Fig. 78, with the little temples or aedicules with their charming gable roofs. It is like a shortened version of the colonnette scheme, and may be how Ruby would have finished them off in the rest of the building if he had carried them up full height.

Now where is the designer in all this? If there was one, he is a disappointment, and if he was replaced, his successors were equally neglectful. I have itemised thirteen major design and structural changes in twenty-three years, or more than one every two years. Does this mean they were changing their architect every other campaign? Either that, or the man employed was not worthy of the title.

And this, I think, may be the real explanation. The client's supervisory staff were clerics, concerned almost exclusively with the arrangement of the plan, the sculpture and the interior. They were uneducated in building matters, and left those difficulties to the men trained to solve them. The major alterations which occur almost every year show it was the builders who changed, and that between the master mason who led the crews and the Chapter there was no one. The master was the architect as we would know him. He made the decisions to change the geometry, the structure or the design. Not only did he control the detailing and the templets for the smaller items, but he controlled the larger ones as well. If we look closely at the changes that were made from one campaign to another, the only thing the client demanded was that the interior follow the one agreed format. And even that instruction was given only in general terms, without specifying either details or dimensions.

We are so used to imposing a heavy control over our buildings that we find it hard to visualise any other system. Art historians on the whole write as men of the twentieth century, with our scientific and control-conscious attitudes. These new facts show that Chartres was the *ad hoc* accumulation of the work of many men. Once our initial dismay is over and we become familiar with the creative possibilities of their ways, we can obtain an altogether new appreciation of mediaeval buildings in their living, growing and organic reality.

It is doubtful whether any of the large builders settled permanently on the construction sites, with the possible exception of some crews of sculptors, or masons working from the quarries. The lack of common detailing and the variety of structural solutions make it clear that builders were mobile, picking up work as they could, bargaining with the client for the best conditions each time, and almost never resident in any one place for long. Such mobility meant that the clergy had a wide range of teams to choose from, encouraging competition and the use of new ideas. However, where the job was a large one, the client either had to limit himself to a big crew or he had to work piecemeal as best he could. Permanence was just not a major characteristic of the mediaeval building trade.

No doubt there were permanent sheds and cranes that were left behind when the contractor moved. But of a settled staff of masons under long-term professional supervision there was none, at least not in the regions bordering on Paris about the year 1200. At the most, the Chapter would have employed a reasonably skilled man to see to the general maintenance of the church and the surrounding buildings, the bishop's palace, the library, clergy's quarters and so on. His role could hardly be more than that of a university architect today who plans the gardens, decides the locations of buildings against one another, organises services like water and sewerage, and general repairs. He may be the man who sought the new contractor after the previous one left, which is also no more than the university architect does today; he selects the private architect for each project, and then more or less leaves him to it.

As a man of my times, I find this *ad hoc* method of contracting a surprising way to go about a great job, but I can see there were sensible historical reasons for it. Project yourself into the last decades of the tenth century. Northern Europe had been under siege for almost two hundred years. Attacked by savage marauders from all directions, by Vikings, Huns and Arabs, what had survived of Roman life and customs collapsed. Orderly government cannot be sustained against constant and successful guerrilla activity. So the communities withdrew into themselves, relying on their own resources to cope with these pirates. They emerged from this isolation only when the pirates themselves settled down and began to accept some of the rural values of civilised law. During these seven generations there were almost no stone structures at all being built north of the Alps and the Pyrenees. Men built in wood. The masons' yards disappeared, and with them the skills they perpetuated. The quarries lay hidden under the weeds.

As conditions improved towards the end of the tenth century, men began to build once more for permanence. But as there were no trained men to engage locally, gangs of masons were called from afar. We have occasional references to some of these, like Robert and his partner who were invited to bring fifty masons from the south of France to Compostela for the great pilgrim church that still stands. There would not have been many of these builders in the early years, and the funds available would not have been as great as they were to become. After all, funding techniques in the middle ages were pretty crude. You could either have it in cash, or borrow it at crippling interest rates. There were no bond issues, forward budgeting or promissory notes, at least not in those years.

So when these rare and costly men were employed to build a new church or abbey, they were able to work only for as long as there was money. When it was spent they left, and the stone walls stood there, covered with straw against the frosts, until another donor gave something substantial. The clergy would then scour the land for a new man to continue the work. And thus it would go on until the entire building had been completed. In the smallest churches as well as the largest, the problem and the answer was the same.

As time passed, local people would be trained, and would set themselves up as contractors, working in the same roving start-and-stop methods begun in the early years. Some large and rich foundations could have been able to employ men continuously until the project was completed. We find this on some royal works, and in a few church projects such as Canterbury Cathedral. But elsewhere, when the money ran out, the builder had to retire.

It need not have been a sudden dismissal; with so many men to pay, the master would have kept his eye on the treasure chest. To be taken unawares by a sudden lack of cash could have cost him weeks of waiting without work while he sought another job. The client may have been obliged to tell the master when he had only enough funds to last another month. The builder could then start looking for the next job, and when the rep from another building site visited Chartres looking for a builder, the master would sign up. Even if more money was received by the treasury after that, the contractor would still have to leave, for he would have committed himself and his men in advance. And who can blame him? It would have been a perfectly reasonable way to resolve the conflict between spasmodic cash flow and the builder's security.

Boom conditions would have added to these problems. For when there was a lot of money available all the builders seem to have expanded their staff to cope with the work, so that the contractual arrangements simply remained the same. During the wealthy period that followed William's conquest of England we find the same annual way of working, and it produced some of the longest churches ever built, including huge projects such as Durham that were completed in less than forty years.

The period around 1200 in northern France was another boom time, producing perhaps half of the religious architecture of the middle ages. What remains are monuments to the enthusiasm and ability to cope in spite of the disorderly supervision.

One of the most important rules seems to have been that when a master took over a job, he did not remove or alter what had already been placed. He might change the shape in the next stone, but what had already been put down was sacrosanct. Maybe it had been blessed, maybe it was just ingrained parsimony—we do not know. But the stones of Chartres show that, once placed, they were not touched again. If masters had always tidied up their predecessor's masonry we would not have this vision into their times. They were more interested in what they were about to do than in the tidiness of the whole. As has been said of other masters, like Raphael and Giotto, they thought that invention was more important than execution.

The second rule was that the templets belonged, absolutely, to the master. This still applies, for in every specification we write that the drawings and other documents remain at all times the property of the architect. It is the only security we possess, as copyright can only with difficulty be made to apply to buildings. Thus the master took his documents with him when he left the job. There are even letters from frantic clients requesting that the architect bring them back, and occasional clauses can be found in later mediaeval contracts defining the ownership of general plans and elevations.

But the templets still belonged to the master. They were usually cut from thin wooden boards of birch or oak, though very large ones might be made out of canvas. The master's office was often called the tracing house, for in it he prepared his drawings, and these templets. He would spread a thin layer of plaster on the floor, and on that would inscribe full size the work that was to be done. When it was large, he would do the same on the sub-floor of the building itself. Some of these traceries have been found in Limoges and elsewhere. If he needed to spring an arch between two piers, recognising that it would be pretty unlikely for any two situations to be identical, he would set out the curves of each one individually, either on the working platform itself or on the floor below. Thus each of the arches would suit the uniqueness of the situation around it. Once templets were cut, they hung in the mason's shed or in the tracing house; when the contractor left, he took them with him.

This is why the new master had to prepare fresh templets on arrival. In vertical elements such as piers and walls and windows he could have just instructed the carpenter to trace the shape directly from the work that had already been done. Sometimes he did not reproduce the earlier shape accurately and the different planes of stonework tell where the joints lie. But in horizontal mouldings no attempt was made to follow the earlier work. I could not find one place in the cathedral where the master continued the exact shape of a moulding begun by his predecessor, except perhaps in some of the string courses inside. Otherwise there was always a change in the templet. And behind the templet lay the geometry of the master, and usually behind that, the foot too. Thus is the master in the end exposed and identified by the methods and rules he follows.

Though in its details the cathedral might be a mess, there is in its completed state a strong feeling of unity. It is a product of its times, and all its parts reflect their common values. The cohesiveness of the work lies in these values rather than in the forms or the detailing. The guidance we expect from the architect was missing, and instead unity was produced in other ways. Somehow we have to acclimatise ourselves to this notion, for we generally believe that the greatest art comes from the individual artist who is allowed to express his individual personality to the full.

This is a renaissance idea, and comes with the changed attitude to the artist embodied in Cellini's autobiography and in Michelangelo's reputation for *terribilità*. Hence we find it hard to conceive of great work without the equally great artist who produced it. Yet there is little evidence for personal genius being held in such exclusive esteem before our times. There were great men, certainly, but their work did not fall apart if other men also had a hand in it. Many paintings, manuscripts and sculpture from all periods are recognisably the work of more than one hand. Theirs was not art by committee, but more by the factory system where each man worked either on what he did best, or simply in sequence, one after another.

What Chartres shows us is that we can be as deeply moved by a work created by many hands as we can by one created by the single genius. Also, the possible monotony where there are too many of one person's clichés is completely avoided. When the contractual system changed after 1250 and one man could be given sole command over a project for decades, we find that the architecture is often less interesting. The system found at Chartres avoids all of that. The dull man is as constrained as the bright one, but at least the greater artist had many opportunities to inject himself into the work, at many levels and places. The result is not one single piece of work, with all the disadvantages that would come if the master was a poor one, but a laminated piece, like a cake in which the pastry is enlivened by many layers of chocolate and other goodies. The result is richer, and if we think our city buildings are getting a little tedious, maybe we should try it ourselves.

The evolution of a great Gothic monument was fluid and organic. It was a process rather than an act, in which the decisions came from the immediate situation rather than from an exactly premeditated plan. The building was a concept in time: the work of the moment, element by element, was the major governing reality.

The completed cathedral is like a biography, for we cannot sweep over a man's life and see it whole until it is completed. Only when the building is finished can we stand aside from the process to experience it in its entirety. Until then the architecture is just the flux of things in time. It is like the growth of a tree from a small seed. We know, and perhaps in one sense the tree knows too, the idealised form it is intended to have: but the accidents and experience of growth, however rational and casual, will alter the ideal to the particular. Shade will force the tree to lean outwards, a stroke of lightning will shatter a branch, a cubby-house will modify its natural order. The mediaeval way of building made it possible for the cathedral, like the tree, to evolve from the generalised concepts of the times into its own rich and particular personality in a way that would not have been possible under our more controlled conditions.

8
MORE ABOUT THE CONTRACTORS

IN NORMAN ENGLAND and in France up to the death of St Louis, nearly every building shows signs of multiple campaigns. I have examined over fifty of them in the Paris basin, and twenty or so in England, and find the same story. Between Blois and Châlons-sur-Marne nearly every building of this period not only shows the same contractual methods, but the presence of many of the same masters.

In the whole area, including the great cathedrals of Reims, Amiens and Paris, there is evidence for no more than twenty-five big crews, which is a finite and comprehensible number. Some tended to work only in the Soissonaise, others chose Paris, and others in the Eure and Loire valleys. But a good dozen seem to have worked across most of the region and, of these, six are found at Chartres—Scarlet, Bronze, Ruby, Rose, Cobalt and Olive. Maybe some day we shall be able to put names to these men.

By studying the master in other buildings we may be able to date works that are at the present moment undatable. The only technique we have today is to look at the entire building and assess where it lies along a pre-prepared theory of evolution where mouldings steadily change towards more advanced and Gothic forms. But I have found one crew after another using the same idea for decades, which makes nonsense of this technique. Scarlet's cornice remained unchanged for eighteen years, and Rose's column bases could not be dated on their own within twenty. But by dividing many buildings up into layers and slotting them into one another, we could produce a more precise dating than we have ever had before, and this would allow us to reconsider our assumptions about the evolution of style on the basis of what actually happened rather than from what we have had to presume.

For example, Bronze's style of work changed subtly during the campaign of 1198, particularly in the way he handled door openings, and his innovative idea, to be discussed later, that windows could be designed from their corners rather than from their faces. The corbels he used about that time become much smaller, and there are other minor changes in his work. We find the same contractor in Laon, where he worked on the western porches. There is doubt about their dates, but if from the windows and the large corbels there we can identify the Bronze at Laon with the earlier Bronze at Chartres, we could perhaps date Laon around 1190. At Reims he finished the doors off the aisles of the nave, and we know from the texts that this must have been some time after 1210. These match his work at Chartres about 1220. Also, his details at Lagny are very similar, and so would presumably be contemporaneous. At Braine to the south of Soissons he may have been the fifth master, and his work there on the stair door lobby is definitely post-1198.

If we are as rigorous about this as nineteenth-century scholars were about royal genealogies, we may ultimately be able to link a program with a name, and give even more reality to our builders. We do have some names, such as those inscribed around the labyrinths of Amiens and Reims. Historians, starting from the assumption that there were permanent workshops established for both buildings with full-time supervision, have called these men the architects.

The labyrinths seem to have had two roles, being not only to exemplify the Way, but also to honour the builders. We can see this in some of the names given to them, for they were not only called 'Jerusalem' but also 'Daedali' after the first architect from mythology, Daedalus. Perhaps we know him better as the first man to fly, but he was also supposed to have invented the builder's tools and to have constructed the labyrinth in Crete, the one with the Minotaur. It is a nice touch that the symbol of man's path to God should also record the names of the men who were able to create the cathedral as the Heavenly Jerusalem on earth, through which the pilgrim could come close to him. The architect certainly had a very high reputation in those days, higher than he has today, and I think that his unique ability to design the House of God had a lot to do with it.

Both the Amiens and Reims labyrinths were set down in the last years of the thirteenth century, sixty or more years after the buildings had been begun, and after most of the work on them had been completed. That in Amiens was designed by Regnault de Cormant, and in the first part he mentions the bishop and king who were alive at the time the cathedral was begun in 1220. He then names only three men in charge for the sixty-eight years up to 1288.

It is hard to believe that so few men could have controlled a big job like this for so long. Amiens Cathedral was one of the largest buildings to be constructed in France, and the Chapter would have naturally chosen experienced and proven men. While they could have been appointed in their forties and all of them could have spent twenty-five years on the site, it would have been unusual. The average working span of senior appointees, as with popes and politicians, is a good deal less than that. However, if the first-named architect, Robert, had been given the job towards the middle of the century, each master would have been in charge for a more realistic period.

There is some confirmatory evidence for this later appointment, not just here, but generally for buildings in the region. After 1250 we find the first recorded names for masons placed in permanent control of works. There is none before. One of the earliest comes from Chartres, a man called Simon Dagon. Was he at that time master for the cathedral as the architect, or just the maintenance man? The layered way in which the gables were being built at that time suggests the latter, but many documents give us this sort of problem. Where they are clear, we find that the architects are either appointed for a specific task, like Martin Chambiges at Troyes, or, like the master of the Royal Works, Henry Yvele, they are hired as consultants, where the pay is quite small, and when work has to be done they are engaged to do it at a higher rate.

At Chartres there is a story that, when Simon Dagon died, his daughter applied for the job, saying it should be hers by hereditary right. The Chapter had to have a special investigation into the matter to determine the problem. If the post had not been a new one she could not have raised the issue, for the succession would have been already long established, by custom.

The buildings show us an ever-changing contractual system around the turn of the century, while the documents tell us that after the 1250s the masters were being given permanent appointments. An examination of the stonework in later buildings does not contradict this, for the joints found in Chartres and elsewhere are absent. Conditions must have changed, but when? During the middle of the boom, or afterwards? Our recent experience with prosperity suggests that that was no time to question fundamental ways of doing things. People just pitch in and do what has to be done.

But once the boom was over, the big teams would not have had enough work. They would have had to cut staff, and we can see one result in the improved workmanship found in most buildings in the 1230s and afterwards. The depression must have had a terrible impact on people, and it would have been natural to seek security and to 'dive for cover'. What would have been better than to look for a permanent position that could keep you going for years, or to reduce the size of the team so that you would not build yourself out of a job so quickly?

It was only after the boom that Gothic took off and spread to other countries. I presume that the better or more ambitious of the laid-off workmen moved out of France in search of work. Some went to England, some to Germany and then to Spain and Italy. The 'Opus Francorum' became the 'Opus Catholicus' of the Christian world.

The first name mentioned in the Amiens labyrinth is Robert de Luzarches. It does not say that he was the first master, but reads:

> Chil qui maistre yert de l'oeuvre
> Maistre Robert estoit nommes
> Et de Luzarches surnommes

which is just, 'He who was master of the works was . . .' When I studied Amiens, I found evidence for sixteen separate campaigns from the footings to the top of the triforium. The place is studded with the same innumerable junctions as Chartres, so neither Robert nor any other person could have had sole architectural control over the lower two storeys.

But if we put Robert in charge about 1250, he could have led the very large campaign that completed the choir. Some of the details in the clerestory are not unlike those in the small chapel added to the southern side of the church in the town from which Robert got his name, and we can date Luzarches from about this time. Was Robert called 'de Luzarches' because he had just finished this chapel when taken on by the cathedral Chapter? Some of the later documents suggest that men's last names changed, and that they were often known as 'the man who we found working at so-and-so before he came here'. If Robert came in 1250, the two other masters mentioned on the labyrinth could have continued Robert's work, including the completion of the transepts and the laying of the labyrinth itself.

The situation at Reims is somewhat similar, though there we may have been given the names of the masters who were responsible for the more important decisions. There is incontrovertible evidence for at least sixteen campaigns from the floor to the triforium. One of the four names on the labyrinth, Jean d'Orbais, is shown with a compass designing the apse, and the inscription reads, 'qu'il encommencea la coiffe de l'eglise'. He is the only master whose time on the job is not mentioned. Jean le Loup is mentioned as working for sixteen years, Gaucher de Reims, who 'ouvre aux vossures et portaulx' for eight, and Bernard de Soissons for an enormous thirty-five. We know that Bernard was still alive in 1287. Subtracting Jean's sixteen years, Gaucher's eight and Bernard's thirty-five from that takes us back to 1228, which is eighteen years after the start of the work. This eighteen years is quite enough to encompass the sixteen or so campaigns from the *ad hoc* period and, by bringing us to 1228 which is about the time the boom burst, marks the moment when the old contractual system may have been replaced by the new.

As with Amiens, the conclusions are the same: there is nothing in either of these inscriptions to contradict the thesis described in this book. The only other important documented exception is the monk Gervase's account of the rebuilding of Canterbury Cathedral after 1174. A French master, William of Sens, won the competition for the job, and worked there for four years before being incapacitated from a fall off the scaffolding. His replacement, another William, continued with the work until it was finished. Canterbury was one of the richest foundations in England, and not unexpectedly the flow of funds matched the number of men working on the job.

But how many men would that be? This is a difficult question to answer, but important. Records from later mediaeval workshops show that large buildings could be put up by only a few men, perhaps a dozen or so, as long as they worked on it for years and years. We know that the two end bays at Troyes Cathedral, plus the uppermost parts of another three, took about a dozen men almost fifty years, which is almost twice as long as we needed for the entire cathedral at Chartres.

Though we have few comparable records for other buildings, there is another way to assess the numbers. By costing the cathedral as if it were built today, using our types of cranes and building methods, but the same materials, glass and sculpture found in the cathedral, the money can be converted into an equivalent number of man-hours. Nearly every piece of material came out of the ground or from the forests, and therefore had to be hewn, axed or quarried by hand. The bulk of the cost was therefore for labour. Extracting timber, and assuming that most of what was left went to pay for labour employed directly by the master contractor, both skilled and unskilled, the money would have paid for more than two hundred men.

This is an enormous number to engage, pay and co-ordinate. Some would have been carters and general labourers, but most would have been organised into gangs each under a foreman. Some gangs spent their time at the quarry, splitting the stone and roughly shaping it. Others finished it into the mouldings and other details required at each specific point. There were laying gangs who placed the stones, and others in between who mixed the cement, lifted and dug, raised the scaffolding and made tea. If there were fifteen gangs, each with a foreman, spread between the quarry, the shop and the site, it would not have been too many. The organisation of so many people was no small task, and would have required quite a large staff besides the master mason himself.

A considerable city project today seldom has more than 150 men at a time on the job, though for short periods towards the end of the work there may be more. However, in modern projects, the workforce has to be increased to produce the services such as lifts and air conditioning, much of which is manufactured in factories far from the site. But in Chartres, all these men were engaged in the common task of cutting and erecting the one material—stone.

Many of these men would have been local. As well as the carters and their teams of oxen, the masons would have used local labour to mix the cement, to carry and to shovel, to move the stone blocks and timbers and all the other manifold unskilled tasks. Nearly everybody in the erection gangs could have come from the town. After a time, some of the villagers may have become proficient in quarrying and roughing the stones and may have joined the builder's team. From evidence of building in Africa and Asia, where modern industrial methods seldom exist, at least 60 per cent of the workforce could have been local, and perhaps more if the people from the area were able, over the years, to acquire some building skills.

This leaves us with about seventy to eighty men in each team who formed the permanent and precious core of skilled men, who stayed with and followed their master from place to place. This is no more than a fair-sized circus today, which is not an unfair comparison. They were itinerants, with firmer loyalties to their mates than to their clients, region or lord. Their strongest attachment was to the master mason himself, whose role must have approached that of a feudal lord. Among these eighty men would be the best masons, at the quarry face and in the shop, and foremen for the erection and laying gangs. These leading hands would have constituted an executive of about twenty key men, without whom no work could have been accomplished.

There was a remarkable permanence about these crews. The parts that are individually carved, such as the capitals, suggest that the leading cutters seldom left one crew to work with another. We find the same personal style in the sculpture and foliage of a team each time it turns up, showing the same permanence in the membership of the team as there is in the institution it forms. They are not, as has at times been suggested, an amalgam of individual masons under the loose supervision of more or less permanent resident masters, but of peripatetic stable groups under the feudatory rule of one leader.

We must not lose sight of the teamwork that is essential to all these great works. There would have been a clear hierarchy of responsibilities in groups as large as this, culminating in the master himself. The organisational achievement of building these cathedrals so quickly is equivalent to the space programs of today. Spending over a million pounds a year and organising two hundred men at a time is no mean task. Every man would have to know what was expected of him. Instructions would have to be clear and unambiguous if the work was to be done economically and with a minimum of waste. Without widespread literacy, drawings would have been intelligible only to the few, and from them would have come all the creative thinking as well as the day-to-day instructions.

Some day we may be able to assess the effect on a small community (for Chartres had only nine thousand inhabitants) of employing so many strangers over such a long period. What happened to their way of life while so much foreign money was being injected into the community, and how did it cope with the many extra services, from accommodation and inns to supplies and whores, that this population demanded? And following this, what happened after a generation had become attuned to these people and the subsidy they brought to the town, when the project was finished and the funds stopped? Was everyone satisfied with the inevitable return to farming and its modest and unpredictable returns, or did the more adventurous, feeling unfulfilled, slip away to other building sites or to the cities? Certainly life was not the same afterwards.

The money which came into these insular agricultural communities could be likened to the flowing rivers of cash the tourists bring into simple economies like Bali or Samoa. The acquisition of money for its own sake takes the place of simple barter and exchange, and the making of it replaces the traditions of a seasonal way of life. To some extent the very act of building the cathedrals to honour their mystic image of God may have helped to destroy the vision. The enormous effort needed to raise the money from an agrarian community more accustomed to barter than to cash would have strained it in many unpredictable ways. Though the cathedrals were the highest expression of the ideals of the period, in being built and paid for they must have so drastically altered the fabric of mediaeval society that the enthusiasm that built them perished.

The funds did not flow in at the same rate for forty years. There were times when twice the average was used per campaign, and other times when they were lucky to find a quarter. The first three campaigns were among the smallest. Considering the enthusiasm the town showed for the work after the fire, this may seem rather small, but remember that the clergy paid for these three years without any assistance from outside sources.

This may have been an old custom, for the same happened at Reims, St Quentin and sundry other places. The pope had to issue a special approval for a Chapter to seek funds outside their own diocese, so it may have been accepted policy for the clergy to show their good intentions and strength of purpose by paying for the first three years out of their own pockets before being granted this honour. Certainly after 1197 the amount of work being done in each campaign jumped dramatically. How was this money raised? As Simson wrote:

It is not easily realised to what extent the religious and economic
spheres interlocked in those days. It is well known how
powerfully the fairs stimulated the development of the medieval
city. The fairs are inseparable from the religious life of the
Middle Ages; indeed they originate in it, and were naturally held
on those feast days that drew the largest crowds of worshipers. In

Chartres the economic life of the entire city centered primarily on four great fairs, which, by the end of the twelfth century, had acquired nearly the reputation of the fairs of Brie and Champagne. Even the manufacture and sale of textiles—the most famous product of the region—profited directly as well as indirectly from the cult of the Sacred Tunic. This is even truer for the producers of victuals—the bakers, butchers, fishmongers—and the merchants of Beauce wine, the quality of which was once famous.

Without the great basilica their professional life would indeed have been hardly imaginable. The fairs of the Virgin were held in the *Cloître* of Notre Dame, that is, in the immediately adjoining streets and squares that constituted the property of the chapter and stood under its jurisdiction. Merchants erected their stands in front of the canon's houses. Fuel, vegetables and meat were sold by the southern portal of the basilica, textiles near the northern one. At night, strangers slept under the cathedral portals or in certain parts of the crypt. Masons, carpenters, and other craftsmen gathered in the church itself, waiting for an employer to hire them. Even the selling of food in the basilica was not considered improper if carried on in an orderly fashion. At one time the chapter had to forbid the wine merchants to sell their produce in the nave of the church, but assigned part of the crypt for that purpose, thus enabling the merchants to avoid the imposts levied by the Count of Chartres on sales transacted outside. The many ordinances passed by the chapter to prevent the loud, lusty life of the market place from spilling over into the sanctuary only show how inseparable the two worlds were in reality.

(1964, pp. 165–7)

The prosperity of the town could not exist without the cathedral, and the pilgrims who were drawn there, like the tourists today, were one major source of cash for the rebuilding. The local guilds are thought to have given money for some of the largest stained glass panels in the cathedral. Local magnates are also recorded as having donated large sums. Count Louis probably provided for the sculpture of the central southern doorway, for he can be seen distributing the loaves of bread to the poor under the feet of the blessing Christ, and again wearing a wreath of flowers among the saved on the lintel.

Modern fund-raising is not very different. Individuals would be asked to pay for specific items, like a pillar here, or a window there, so they could see where their cash was being used, and their pride in what they had accomplished would spur others on.

But probably the greatest source of income was the relics, and in this Chartres was particularly fortunate in having the most celebrated ones associated with the Virgin, that of her tunic and the head of her mother. Relics, gruesome as some were, were big business in the middle ages. The Venetians, among the canniest financiers of the time, accepted the Crown of Thorns as full security for an enormous loan. It was not only worth money itself, but like all valuable capital was capable of raising great sums of money for its possessor. In one year, exceptional admittedly, we know that the relics of St Thomas produced an income of close on a quarter of a million pounds for the see of Canterbury.

So when funds were required, the relics were taken to the other areas, and to other countries. If the relics produced miracles on the way, so much the better. We have many stories about the ones they did produce, and clearly they were spectacular enough to entice funds from everywhere. Even during the war between the French and the English the kings of both sides were prevailed upon to give to Chartres, so the Virgin might look a little more kindly on their particular side.

But, above all, as Simson says, Chartres 'was the work of France and of all of France, as no other great sanctuary had been before. The cathedral windows bear magnificent testimony to the national effort'. (1964, p. 180) Besides the donations made by the guilds, we find those of the ancient feudal houses of the Ile-de-France: Courtenay, Montfort, Beaumont, Montmorency. The counts of Chartres, and especially the royal family, made great contributions. The entire composition of the northern façade was given by Blanche of Castille, mother of St Louis, while all the corresponding windows in the opposite transept were donated by one of her more implacable enemies, Peter of Dreux, duke of Brittany.

The bulk of the money raised went on the building itself, and probably the largest single item was cartage. The slow lumbering wagons drawn by teams of local oxen would have taken a full day to draw a load from the quarry to the cathedral 12 kilometres away. A young boy could have helped his father cart the first load after the fire,

79 The leaves carved at the tops of the solomonic shafts supporting the statues in the embrasures of the doorways.

grown up watching the outline of the new work rise slowly above the walls of the town, and retired as the speed of building declined after the vaults had been finished. It was truly the work of a lifetime!

The glass which has occupied so much attention, and which covers nearly an acre of window area, cost only 10 per cent of the total, while the sculpture which so enthrals and moves us cost less than 3 per cent. Surprising as this may seem, this figure is if anything over generous. The sculpture was costed after talking to artists to see how long it would take them to carve a figure, and then the time was doubled. Similarly the labour cost was taken at the normal rate for a skilled man, and then doubled. Yet we know from mediaeval accounts that sculptors were paid little more than other skilled carvers. They were not a race apart as they are today. The middle ages had no concept of the artist as a special sort of man, as we do. The post-renaissance belief in individual genius had not entered their minds. They were paid well, but in proportion. Our exaggerated claims for artistic effort were happily unknown.

I analysed the carving in the building in two stages: first the capitals and other mouldings with leaves and berries on them, and afterwards the figures. I was fortunate in having the help of twenty English students for one glorious summer fortnight. We split into groups, and armed with binoculars and pencils studied different parts of the building until we knew them intimately. I co-ordinated what they

80 Foliage and *fleurs de lis* on the panels under the piers of the north porch. The lower row is by Bronze and the upper by Ruby.

found, and realised that if I had spent the same time doing each piece of work myself the sharper edges of memory would have faded before I would have been half-way through. With them I was able to see simultaneously through my helpers' eyes and gather a total picture.

We were able to distinguish different modes of carving, though we could not say whether they represented people or gangs. I gave them names, like 'Lobelia' for the mason who carved intricate and highly-stylised lobed leaves, 'Pruner' for the group who pruned a part of each branch and carved their stalks with an octagonal section rather than a round one, and so on. Because I had by then established which teams had worked there, I was able to apportion these carvers among the contractors. This showed one very interesting thing: that the same hand could be seen carving in an unvarying style over very long periods of time. Thus 'Flap' and 'Rocky' made almost identical capitals for Ruby in 1199, 1206, 1211 and 1216. Seventeen years with almost no change in the shape of the leaves and the arrangement of the capital was not uncommon, and showed that though the style of the period as a whole might be evolving slowly, and that there may have been gradual modifications within the teams themselves, among the individuals there was often no change at all.

When we think about it, this is not strange. For the individual to change, he must either belong to an anti-traditionalist society like our own or be subjected to strong outside influence. Mediaeval society naturally minimised both these things. So the individual tended to remain within the mould that had formed him in his early years. Changes may have come about as one man was supplanted by a younger with more up-to-date views.

For example, on the side of one of the lintels of the north porch there is a sculpture by one of Olive's men that can be dated 1210. It is a tiny figure, surmounted by a gable. Up the sides of the gable there are tiny flames. In architecture these flames do not appear until the 1250s, in the Chartres transept gables, in Sées and Paris. What happened in the meantime? Perhaps this figure had been carved by a gifted young man just completing his apprenticeship who had been allowed to try out his idea in this remote corner. Much later he may have risen through the ranks to become the master, and was then able to realise his youthful dreams by bringing the flames out of the smaller items to be displayed in the most public manner possible.

So new ideas in architecture may have been conceived many decades earlier in the youth of the contractor. There is a similar example in Durham, where they built the first rib vaults. Of the nine contractors working there, three and maybe as many as four were prepared to put ribs under the vaults. The rest were not, and tried to sabotage this idea wherever possible. Nevertheless the ribs got there. The intriguing question remains, that if so many of the contractors were working towards ribs, which was a completely novel idea at that time, why had the first man to have had that idea not been able to build them years before? Some may have been destroyed, but I think it more likely, as with the flames on the gables, that ideas moved slowly within the team, and even when they got to the top they still had to find the opportunity. The master with the brilliant new thought has to be in the right place at the right moment to introduce it, and by then it may have been current in many men's thinking for a decade or more. After all, it was no good wanting to put in ribs when you were only being given footings to do, for you would never have had the chance.

Having isolated the leaves in the capitals, I was ready to try apportioning the sculptures. I immediately found that about 15 per cent of them could be attributed to this crew or that from the leaves carved on them. Another 40 per cent could then be given to one crew or another, using the normal techniques of connoisseurship. This was enough to show that the bulk of the sculpture was the work of the contractor's men, not of specialists. One day they would be turning out a St John or a Maurice, and the next a cornice or a sill moulding.

Do not think that carving mouldings was demeaning. Some were incredibly intricate and difficult. Take for example the round mouldings at the bottom of the columns, which cover the transition from the cylinder to the square of the base. The shape of these tori was gradually changing at this time, and the scotia was being twisted around and the opening into it squeezed shut.

81 The head of the soldier-saint, Maurice. He is the intellectual and philosopher compelled to carry arms.

It was a slow evolutionary process that began about 1180, when the static Roman base began to change. This is the base on the left (in Fig. 82). Over two generations, the scotia was twisted round its axis, as though it was responding to the pressures coming on to it from the top of the building by twisting outwards and up. This process was completed about 1230, when the opening into the scotia snapped shut altogether. The torus had begun to change with the boom, and finished with the bust. It began looking like rings tied round a shaft, and ended like a plumber's cover mould. Both were static forms, unlike the intermediate period when the moulding seemed to pulsate with inner life. The history of this moulding seems to reflect the spirit within the community that produced the cathedrals, opening and stretching with the people's enthusiasm, and closing shut when it failed.

Put yourself in the place of the mason carving one of these scotias. You have a curved hollow to cut out, with a slot to work

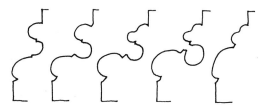

82 The evolution of the 'pressurised' torus between the years 1180 and 1230.

through that is only a centimetre or so wide. You have to get your chisel into this opening, and without damaging the edges carve a perfect curve from within the stone. And remember that we are working in one of the hardest and most brittle stones available, limestone. Nothing has been skimped in these bases. It must have taken the mason a great deal of time and patience to cut. It was a costly item, and could have been carved only by one of the best men in the team.

Thus the most skilled masons in the crew were making these mouldings when needed, sculpture when there was a call for any, and at other times would have to be content with plain walling. They could not have had our genius-complex, for they worked at what had to be done each day, without conceit.

Some of the sculpture may have been done by specialists or wandering craftsmen unattached to the gangs, but on the whole we can say that if only 3 per cent of the building cost went on sculpture, there would be room in France for only one or two gangs of specialists. When we think of the variety of figure work and the number of individuals who must have been involved, this number of men could have been found only within the building teams, unless most of them spent the bulk of their time unemployed.

On the whole, the sculptors do not seem to have felt they were unusually endowed men doing a special kind of job. They were proud, but as craftsmen who could turn their hand to anything. They probably had the natural unselfconsciousness that is today found only in traditional communities.

During the height of the boom the masters seem to have worked as if they were going to be employed for ever, and as if every building would go on getting taller until it reached heaven itself. Not one of the ambitious proposals begun at this time was completed. The parish church of St Pierre in Chartres is one of the longest in France. Yet in spite of its length, where the thirteenth-century triforium butts into the earlier tower at the western end the mouldings were extended into it as if the tower was to have been pulled down so that even more bays could be added to the nave. At Gallardon, east of Chartres, the clerestory windows in the choir were continued behind the tower in anticipation of being extended to the west. Yet both the tower and the Romanesque nave would have had to have been demolished to make this happen. Not only did the master expect it would be torn down, but confidently prepared for it. No one could wait until it could be done, it had to be prepared for now and at once. They were truly in the grip and frenzy of their enthusiasm.

At Laon they kept on adding storeys to the towers, each thinner and less stable than the last. And even when they had reached the top of these teetering edifices they continued the treads of the stairs another ten risers or so as if trying to leap into the next storey before even the one below had had time to settle. They seemed to be working feverishly, piling ever more levels of precarious masonry over stones that were already strained. Everything was in anticipation of the next step. To stop was unthinkable.

But when it did, in the 1230s, the unparalleled optimism, that had spurred them so far and had stimulated them to design as few men have before or since, split apart. The men who could scurried for cover, and the security of modern professionalism took over. It is safer, but has it, do you think, produced better architecture?

9
THE GEOMETERS

IMAGINE A MODERN building designed successively by Le Corbusier, Mies van der Rohe and Frank Lloyd Wright. Corb's foundations for his massive *pilotis* would be simplified and abstracted by Mies into a lighter framed arrangement. Wright, finding this on arrival, would tend to soften the rigorous logic of the earlier parts with a more complete geometry and with softer decorative forms. The major contributor to the design would inevitably have been Corb, and the other masters would have had to adapt themselves to the policy outlined in his plan. And, of course, if it had been the other way round, Wright's intricate geometric sense would have set the pattern for all to follow. Even though much would have depended on the first master's plan, later men would have had quite some latitude within it to express their own ideas.

If you think the result would inevitably have to be chaotic, you would be wrong. Whenever one of these highly creative individuals has designed an addition to an older building he has worked with care and sympathy to preserve what he thought best in the earlier work. It is one of the hallmarks of the creative man of any age that he is sensitive to the challenge of his setting. Creative work without some sense of unity through it is not art, which is why even under mediaeval contracting conditions the masters developed a technique to ensure some sort of unity.

Imagine that their way of working is not something new, but has been happening for generations, and that Corb and the others grew up and fulfilled their apprenticeship knowing they would have to work this way. Every time they designed something they would be aware that nothing of theirs need be final or binding on the future. Every decision was for the moment and for the extent of their own participation. Beyond that they were powerless.

83 The curves of geometry are nowhere more apparent than in the chapels, here seen looking directly downwards.

They would be quite accustomed to moving on to new jobs, and to picking up the threads each time. Each would have been to some extent influenced by the ideas put up before him. After Bronze began the window wall, his successors would have reacted to it, and perhaps, after waiting to see what it would look like, a few may have incorporated the idea into their own repertoire. Ruby seems to have taken it up, for he used the twin lancets in his winning design for the clerestory competition just ten years later. He still interpreted the idea his own way by framing the outside of the window with shafts where Bronze had none, capping it with a huge rose under a round arch.

But for most of the time the master's freedom was heavily circumscribed by what had already been built, so his major training lay in learning how to adapt himself to circumstances. Dull complacency is not possible under this sort of stimulation. No one can be insensitive to the work of others when he is forced to adapt each time, though the master may have stuck to the same shapes for mouldings and other

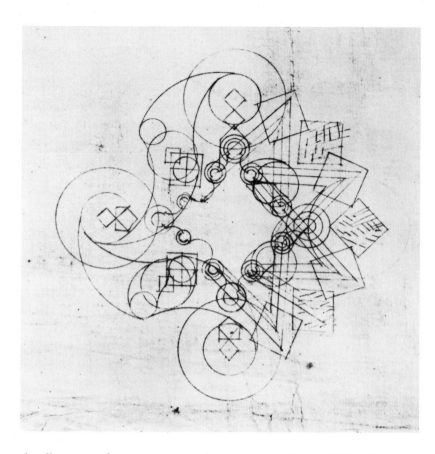

84 Mediaeval drawing for a pulpit (from F. Bucher, *Journal of the Society of Architectural Historians*, 1968, pp. 49–71).

details year after year to retain some certainty within the ever-changing world around him.

Today under these conditions our adjustments would be made by eye, using our artistic sense, but in an age when every piece is evolved by geometry, the adaptations would be geometric too. There was no room in the 1200s for the visual adjustments we find in Classical architecture, like thicker columns against the corner with a narrower bay next to it, or tapering shafts and the swelling called entasis part-way up that were all invented to aid the eye. The mediaeval cathedral was not built to be seen from man's viewpoint, but from the pure and universal view of God himself. Perspective and other optical refinements were irrelevant to people who believed they were building a slice of Paradise. They only had to have the knowledge and understanding of God's purpose to be able to duplicate it in architecture, in music and in life. They came to believe that only through discipline, be it monastic, scholastic or geometric, could the truth be reached. In architecture we can clearly see how all-pervasive this belief was, for there is not one decision that was not made through geometry.

Geometry was not a tyrant, for they had choices and no doubt the master let the artist in him guide his choice of the geometry he used. When Ruby was working in the nave aisles, he made the window openings equal to the width of the piers. This was a wonderful decision. It set up a contrapuntal positive–negative rhythm down the nave between piers and windows. The way that the mass that holds up the structure is set against the void that illuminates it is very beautiful.

The piers in Chartres were among the largest ever built, and this made it possible for Ruby to work it this way. In most other buildings the piers were just single drums without the attached shafts used at Chartres, and if he had used this idea everywhere his spaces would have been ill lit indeed. Elsewhere he may have derived the window from something else, for it had to be linked to other elements. All the work at Chartres shows that nothing was designed in isolation.

Besides the window, Ruby made a number of other decisions in this campaign. He fixed the height of the string course on the inside and the drip mould outside, located the glass within the wall and its sill height above the floor. Before making any decisions he would have studied the area around about, and measured it carefully. He would have noticed that the width of the pier was almost exactly eight of his feet, which was a whisker larger than the modern English foot. Using one-third of this as a module, he made the height of the string course four

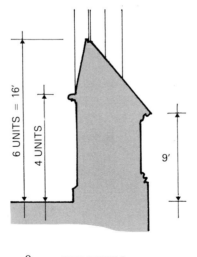

85 Section through the nave wall showing the modules used by Ruby.

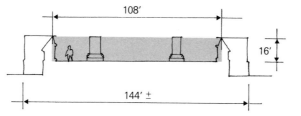

86 Cross-section of the nave with the overall proportions used by Ruby.

units, the height of the sill six and the window width three. On the outside he set the drip mould at 9 feet from the floor.

When I measured the distance from the face of one stained glass window to the other I found it was 108 feet, and so I drew the little section (Fig. 86) to see what else this gave me. Within a few inches he would have discovered that the overall width of the nave would have measured 144 of his feet (remember it had originally been placed by someone else), and that it formed a ratio to the gap between the glazing of 4 : 3 I could now begin to see what Ruby might have been working to. The rectangle within the interior, defining that dark and sombre enclosure bounded by the solids of the floor and the walls up to the glass line and shaded on the drawing, measured 108 by 16 feet. This is the ancient pythagorean ratio 27:4, credited with many sublime qualities partly because of the beautiful looking relationship it forms of three to the power three against two to the power two, which is mathematically like this — $3^3 : 2^2$.

So it seemed that Ruby could be interested in powers. With this hint, I examined the rest of his work. The building width of almost 12^2 might have started him off, for he followed that with a drip height measuring 3^2 and a sill set at 4^2 feet up. The next elements to be fixed by Ruby were the string courses under and over the triforium. The heights of these strings worked neatly to 49 and 64 feet, which is of course 7^2 and 8^2. I was struck by the series this was beginning to form in which he had already used the squares of 3, 4, 7, 8 and 12. What of the other numbers in between, the 5, 6, 9, 10 and 11? I found the 5^2 in half the space across the nave between the faces of the walls above the aisle capitals. This had been located by Ruby in his 1202 campaign. The others are not to be found, as Ruby was at no time able to locate any of the other vertical dimensions.

But I could make a guess at what he might have done. The 6^2 may have located the centre points for the curved part of the arcade arches,

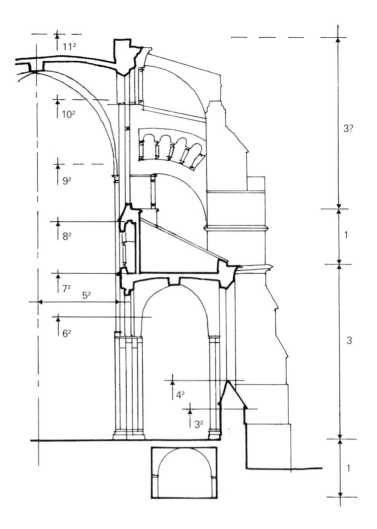

87 Section of the cathedral
showing the possibilities in
Ruby's system of squares. On
the right is shown his second
system using the crypt as a
module.

above the stilting or vertical section which rises for about a metre
above the capitals. 9^2 could have located the springing for the high
vaults about 3 feet higher than now, and 11^2 would have fixed the boss
of the high vaults, even if they were to be 7 feet higher.

Until we find Ruby using all these steps in a continuous series in
another building, there is no way of knowing whether this is a good
guess or not. But it certainly fits all we know of the masters' search for
pattern in their geometry.

Pattern, and the beautiful intricacies it creates, was one of the most
important manifestations of the mediaeval spirit. It occurs everywhere
we look: the leaves on a panel, the hem of a gown, the great coruscating
rose windows and every part of the geometry itself. Cobalt's was if

anything over-precise, Bronze's may have been variable, and Ruby's was predictably less arty than the others, but all the masters show the same extraordinary passion for it. We can see it most clearly in some of the later medieval drawings.

In those few places like the bosses where form and nature could be brought together, we always find below the profusion of leaves and berries a severe geometric discipline. There is one of Cobalt's which can be divided into four identical quadrants. The branch forms a strong motif linking one group with another, while following the arcs of circles drawn against the perimeter. The berries are like stops marking the gaps between the circles. The underlying geometry is like the quatrefoil window tracery from the next generation. Here in 1207 the mason has hidden under his leaves the formal patterns that will later be openly expressed in tracery.

Another design by Ruby is based on interlocking squares rather than on circles. In this arrangement four leaves lie over another four with eight berries filling the spaces in between them. But the berries are not at all accidental, for each marks one of the salient points in the two systems of geometry which outlined the leaves on the boss. This

88 One of Cobalt's bosses where the pattern fits between an octagon star and four circles. The width of the ribs determined the size of the centre from which every other part was evolved.

89 Another boss in the sanctuary is contained within a double geometry—by one of Ruby's gangs.

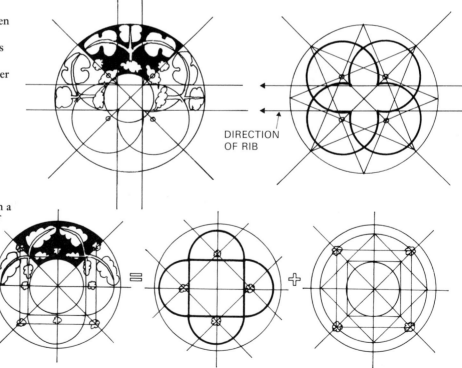

DIRECTION OF RIB

geometry is very like the twelve big circles that surround the western rose.

We even find that pattern pervades structure. Ruby designed the layout of the eastern buttresses above the walkway. When he arrived, he found that the base on which he was to design the next stage of the

90 The large buttress between the sanctuary and the chapels, within which lies a staircase. The blind doors were probably for builders' access during construction.

91 The large buttresses between the sanctuary and the apse chapels were designed contrapuntally, as if this interlacing pattern of numbers would hold it together structurally.

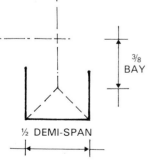

buttress was, thanks to Bronze's straightening of the axis, longer and thinner on the north, and wider and squatter on the south. I find his solution quite extraordinary for its entirely unstructural way of resolving a structural problem. He repeated the ratios he had used on other occasions of 3:8 for the depth of the buttress and 1:2 for the width. But he founded these ratios on quite different dimensions. On the south the depth was calculated from the bay and the width from the half-span, while on the north he puts them round the other way and used the half-span for the depth and the bay for the width. He just swapped them over.

Now this may be poetry, but it is not engineering. One side has been balanced against the other by reciprocating magic formulae: like nailing a horseshoe over the front door and mistletoe over the back. We can see that he has made a pretty pattern, and for us that is all there is. But surely Ruby believed that the pattern was something more besides? It was a sign that he had tapped a deeper consciousness that would guarantee stability. The choice of the appropriate pattern seems to have invoked other greater powers, like a pact with God in which the master finds the right arrangement and in return God agrees to maintain the building in its place. In this sense geometry is both a sacrament and a vision into the Divine.

We are lucky to have so many of Ruby's decisions, for they give us a precious insight into his thinking. The aisle windows, the arrangement in the triforium and the clerestory are largely his work, and this makes him one of the three most influential men to have worked on the cathedral. Bronze is another, and the third must be the first master, Scarlet.

There are only three vertical dimensions that can be safely ascribed to Scarlet, and the most important is the floor-level. Now anyone can put down a floor, but in a sacred building its position is of the utmost importance. The floor lies over the crypt, and though we do not really know why these lower chambers were built, they were certainly not for burials, though people were occasionally entombed there. The word comes from the Latin for 'hidden', and I think that in the chthonic sense it represented the underground level of spirituality, the deep abyss of the cave and the womb or feminine side of the unconscious. This might then explain why crypts that were popular in Romanesque buildings went out of fashion at this time, for, as the worship of the Virgin became established, she provided the balance to the all-male

Trinity that had been lacking before. The psychological need for the womb-cave under the church disappeared as the rituals centred on the Mother's altar became predominant within it.

The floor marks the boundary between the subterranean feelings associated with the crypt and those of the earthly plane. Below the floor lies concealed the foundations, and that sub-structure that supports the multifarious activities of man. It represents the left hand of heaven where the vault and the sky denote the right. This plane of change is therefore hardly unimportant.

Scarlet located the floor through the triangular construction in Fig. 93. By taking the floor of the crypt as the base for the cathedral, he implied that the crypt was the true foundation for the church. If we need a proof for this, it is that the top of the octagonal footings under the piers are a few centimetres higher on the north side of the building than on the south, because both were measured from the floor of the crypt, and on the north the crypt is a little higher than the south.

Separate measurements were taken on each side of the building, and

92 One of the chapels in the crypt.

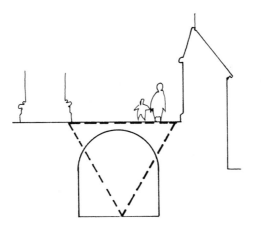

93 The equilateral triangle, with each half-side measuring 10 feet positioned the floor-level from the crypt.

even if the floor was to end up with a tilt, it was more important to express the relationships truly on each side of the building than to have an absolutely level floor. Doesn't that remind you of the reasons for the three squashed bays at the western end of the nave?

From the floor upwards, every level of the northern side of the building was set a few centimetres above that of the south. The level of one side was never checked against the other across the open space of the nave, which shows that they made their vertical measurements separately on each side. They used long rods, probably of wood, and placed them vertically on the footing course in each bay. The length of the rod was the module or unit which could be used in a number of places. Technically it was the easiest and most accurate way to build vertically, and we have seen that this is also the way Ruby set out the aisle windows.

Never forget that a building site is anything but a tidy spot. The ground is littered with stones and timbers waiting to be erected. The walls are covered with scaffolding and there would be ladders and cranes all over the place. Some parts would be higher than others, and the general appearance would be of a forested hilltop after a bombardment. When setting out a piece of geometry in plan it is relatively easy to stretch lengths of string across the site, and to pull them tight. Quite complicated figures can be constructed in this way, even on platforms set high up in the air. But to do this vertically is altogether another matter, as you can imagine. This is why the rod, and the module it represents, was the simplest, and hence the commonest, way to establish heights. The use of difficult geometry vertically, let alone some people's theories that the cathedrals were set out directly from solid figures, was out of the question.

Returning to Scarlet—he came back to the site in 1200 and made two important changes. In the east he eliminated Ruby's drip and began the wall under the walkway, and in the east he sat another course of stonework over Ruby's sill to raise it to a new level. His geometry eliminated poor Ruby's, though his sills can still be seen under Scarlet's more bulbous ones. The new glass line was placed the same height above the floor as the floor is above the crypt. Straightforward use of the rod again. The geometry of the arrangement would look like two triangles joined together.

The length of the base of the triangle is 10 feet times two. The two and the three in the triangle remind me of the first numbers he had used in the formal layout for the cathedral represented in the twin towers and the three chapels. Ten is, as Aristotle said, 'the total of all things embracing the entire world.' In it One, symbol for the Qualified Principle, is joined with Zero, the Unqualified Principle, into a statement that represents the All united in itself.

In the symbolism of the triangle the apex represents the First Principle, below and from which are generated the aspects of the First Duality. There is a mean implied in any duality which is the compromise that follows any confrontation. This mean is not of either party to the conflict, but must be what results from it. In the triangle, the horizontal represents the duality which came when God began the

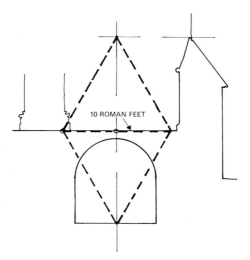

10 ROMAN FEET

94 The double triangle relates the two floors to the light-source above the sills.

creation of the world, while the vertical, the mean, would be the Divine Principle made manifest in the Creation. This may be the meaning given in the middle ages to the $\sqrt{3}$ ratio.

When the triangle is inverted, it represents the consequences of duality, which resulted in the formation of the world as we know it. This is epitomised by the number four and the earth we stand on. As Christ said to Peter, 'on thee shall I build my church', being a canny pun on Peter = Pietro = rock. This is why Scarlet placed the lowest point of this figure, forming the last and fourth point of the diamond, on the floor of the crypt, for it represents the rock as the foundation of the church as building, and of the church as God's representative on earth.

This arrangement has other meanings too. The window-sill above which light enters the church lies on the upper point of the diamond. As Suger tells us, the degree to which a thing resembles God shows how present he is in it, and so determines its place in the hierarchy of beings. This may be why light became so important in the middle ages. It was sublime, and made the mystic reality palpable to the senses. By analogy, light and the Godhead are conjoined at the apex. The mobility of light is poised against the solidity of darkness: for the floor of the cathedral lies between the light and the dark rock on which the crypt and the cathedral is built. This mean represents the duality which came from the First Principle, while it also divides the upper and lower hierarchies. It is itself a duality.

No other master had the same theological profundity as Scarlet. Bronze by comparison was an innovator, in practical rather than in philosophic things. Amongst other things Bronze was one of the few masters to use the fascinating ratio of the golden mean. For the builder, the most important function of φ, as we write the golden mean, is that if he uses it consistently he will find that every subdivision, no matter how accidentally it may have been derived, will fit somewhere into the series. It is not too difficult a ratio to reproduce, and Bronze could have had the two arms of his metal square cut to represent it. All he would then have had to do was to place the square on the stone and, using the string drawn between the corners, relate any two lengths by φ. Nothing like making life easy.

When Bronze came to Chartres for the first time in 1195, he found the footings for some of the nave piers and some of the walls already in place. He made a few small modifications, reducing the width of the

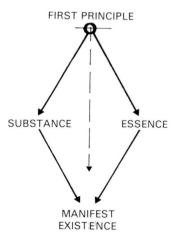

FIRST PRINCIPLE

SUBSTANCE   ESSENCE

MANIFEST
EXISTENCE

95 In the symbolism of the triangle lies both the act of Creation and its consequences; both the process and its manifestation.

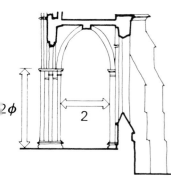

96 The spaces of the aisles form golden mean ratios in all directions, determined by Bronze in the plan, and later in the placement of the capital.

97 Section through aisle of nave shows Bronze's use of the golden mean (φ) in the spaces between the stonework.

aisle slightly and increasing the size of the pier, so that above the torus the most important relationships were to lie in the spaces between the masses, rather than within the masses themselves. Scarlet had worked to axes and built outwards from them, and thus space was for him incidental. Bronze more or less preserved these axes and the general form of the piers and walls begun by Scarlet, but with minor changes that made spaces more important than solids.

The relationship Bronze introduced into the nave was simple: the gap between the piers as seen from the nave was to relate to the space of the aisle as $\varphi:2$. Now occurred one of those pieces of utter good fortune that we should not have to take into account, but which do in fact often bear a large responsibility for the greatness of many works of art. I can hear it being said that a place with the mystique of Chartres would bring the best out in its men and that we should not have to talk of luck. But even these powers would not have determined which, of all nine masters, was to be entrusted with the task of fixing the height of the arcade piers. The choice could only have been the luck of the draw, and it happened to be Bronze. It could have been anybody, and obviously in some buildings was, for few arrangements are as pleasing as here, in the sense that plan and elevation are so perfectly integrated.

When he returned in 1205 he made the height of the arcade capitals twice the length of the rod that fitted in between the piers. Too easy. But in the process not only was he extracting a unit from the plan to make the elevation, but it was also the unit he had himself established ten years before. It meant that the opening down the aisles, which is what the eye records, formed a φ rectangle. As we walk down the cathedral we inhabit one of the most perfect spaces imaginable. It feels at peace, and utterly stable. I am sure the reason is the harmony of the proportions used. It is an amalgam of Scarlet's centres and piers, with Ruby's string course and windows that were derived from the piers, and Bronze's spaces.

It is interesting to see that in the actual calculation of the sequence of dimensions there is a small error. After Bronze had modified the plinths in the second campaign, later masters established the actual size of the pier in the torus mould. The piers are thus a little smaller than he would have made them, and so the space between them is about an inch larger than he intended in 1195. But the rods were always measured to what had been built, and never to what might have been intended many years earlier. The φ relationship to the capitals is thus exactly true as we see it, even if the capital is a little higher than he would have made it had the piers not been reduced. Practice comes before theory, and the real before the drawing, every time.

Bronze repeated this idea in the aisle vaults, though only at the eastern end. The nave formwork had been erected by Cobalt in 1207 as twice the module of a typical bay. But in the choir the formwork is Bronze's, set to a height of three of the modules used for the capitals. By simply using one unit extracted from the plan he created a rich set of interrelated proportions, involving permutations of 1, 2 and 3 with the golden mean.

The high vaults were also located by Bronze in the 1220s, where we again find the same ratios being used. Three times the bay located the under side of the vault from the floor, and three times the span placed the top of the vault from the crypt. From the bay came the visible internal form, while the span located the overall envelope of the cathedral. In the adaptation he had made to Scarlet's first plan in 1195, he had worked to an overall length of the cathedral of twice that height from the crypt. Like Scarlet, he had set the great mass of the cathedral within a double box—though the parts located by his box were not the same as those used by Scarlet, discussed on p. 163.

While each master used a rod of his own choosing to locate the verticals, there were also a number of commonly accepted concepts, such as that of the cruciform church plan and the three-storey elevation that affected everybody's imagination. Compare the solid sense given by the enclosing walls round the aisles with the open fretwork of the flyers to the clerestory. One is earthbound and the other insubstantial, and some of the proportions show that the masters deliberately divided the building into these zones for theological as well as architectural reasons.

For example, if the height from the floor to the walkway round the nave roof is divided into seven modules, then three will give the height to the floor of the triforium. You will remember that this ratio is the same 7:3 used in the plan between the span and the bay. What other parts might have been picked up in this series if one master had had command of the entire building? Another module, a favourite with a number of masters, was the height from the floor to the crypt. Three of these were employed to fix the height of the exterior triforium walkway, plus one to the clerestory and another three to the walkway around the roof of the choir. This can be seen in Fig. 87.

The dark band of the triforium may have been seen as that indefinable region between earth and heaven, the zone of the stars and the empyreum that separates the mortal from the celestial. Is this why there are five columns in the nave triforium, for the five planets? Does the lower string course in some way represent the moon, which may be why Ruby made its height 7^2 feet? And the upper one alongside the clerestory represent the sphere of the fixed stars, being the eighth ring in the Ptolemaic cosmos, and made 8^2 feet high? Is this why the top of the clerestory rose was placed as high above the floor as the space between the aisle windows? It would have created literally a glass box within the cathedral. I feel there are many spiritual and symbolic meanings hidden in these ratios, and only time and more information will help us to unravel them.

Over the years other rods were cut for the triforium and the clerestory, leaving a trail of interlaced modules woven across the façade. Each repetition added something memorable, and in the growing wealth of pattern within pattern gave it that familiar air of magic. The upper parts grew from the lower. How like nature itself, where every branch and leaf is dependent on the trunk which supports it and the roots which give it nourishment. From the subtlety of the first plan and the happy modifications made in the next year came a

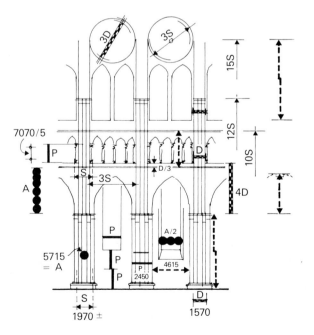

98 Elevation of a typical bay, showing some of the modules used. The dashed line is the bay space and the dot marked A the aisle. P is the pier width, S the centres between the pier's shafts and D the drum of the pier. These four have been used to determine a large part of the elevation.

delectable blend of elements which, coming from the one source, ensured unity in spite of the pervading variety.

Here, then, is the key to mediaeval unity. It lies in the method, and made the permanent architect unnecessary. Having to start every operation from the existing stones bred a sympathy for the work of one's predecessor, while the geometric disciplines used on the elevations enforced some sort of unity even under the least sympathetic masters. One of these disciplines was to separate the geometry for the decorative elements from the structural ones, and to keep sacred symbols distinct from both. We can see they did this in the ratios employed on the decorative string courses, while structural parts, the attic cross walls and the flyers have their own system of geometry, no matter who the master was. He may have organised it in his own way, but he would still keep structure separate from decoration.

All of these aspects, be they structural or decorative, were evolved out of the axial dimension through the bay and span. But as the building rose and these two dimensions were transformed into the elements and details which determined the height, the axial lengths were lost. However, in the high vaults, and especially in the roof, the axes were again used as a kind of summary. The bay relates to the spans as 3:7, and when Bronze raised the roof, he tied the ridge into the first dimension in a quite magnificent way—for this height was made three times the span, which automatically also made it seven times the bay.

Scarlet would have created his envelope differently, for he intended to make the height of the vaults half the length of the 241 foot diamond in the Creation Figure. The present vaults are a lot lower than this, but we know what he intended, because in 1215 he began the western rose, both designing it and starting the lower part of the opening. The top of the rose is a metre higher than the vaults, except for the western bays in which the vaults have been stepped up to suit the rose. Scarlet built the lowest stones of the ribs for these vaults in the same year, and you can in places see where the curve has been altered to lower the pitch when the formwork was built in later years. There had to be a long pause between starting the springing and building the vaults, for they first completed the clerestory walls and then put the roof over it before forming for or erecting the stone ribs and cells. It made the work more stable and kept out the rain. Hence there was ample time to reconsider

99 The western rose, by Scarlet in 1215.

Scarlet's tall vaults, and for some less daring master to reduce them.

Scarlet's western rose is a fabulous piece of design. The rose was a set piece, like the cadenza within the concerto, where the master could exercise his virtuosity to his heart's desire. As with Scarlet's other designs, there is more than pattern in his work. There are thirty-seven openings in the rose, which is not uncommon. What is unusual is the way these openings seem to have been given meanings in relation to other parts of the design.

100 The six times 6 magic square of the Sun:

Total number of figures	36
Sum of rows & diagonals	111
Sum of each block of four	74
Sum of perimeter numbers	370
Sum of all numbers	666
Opposite pairs (e.g. light shading)	74
Diagonal opposites (e.g. medium shading)	37
Perimeter pairs (e.g. dark shading)	37

and there are many other patterns around all the axes of symmetry that can be explored.

6	32	3	34	35	1
7	11	27	28	8	30
19	14	16	15	23	24
18	20	22	21	17	13
25	29	10	9	26	12
36	5	33	4	2	31

Thirty-seven is the thirteenth prime, and there are thirteen months in the lunar year. Multiply this by the Trinity and you get 111, which is itself the Trinity again, and is the sum of each line on one of those fascinating arrangements known as magic squares. These squares are grids of numbers in which every row, horizontally, vertically, and diagonally, will add up to the same number. The six times 6 magic square sums to 111, and is known as the square of the Sun. In gematria, 111 is the total of the letters for the spiritual marriage of Christ and his Mother as 'Jesus Maria'. Six times this (and the rose is based on a twelve-pointed star) is the number of the Beast, the word for which occurs *thirty-seven* times in the Book of Revelations. As Michell remarks:

> This detail is not without a significance in canonical literature, for works such as Revelation were planned so that the balance of elements within the various episodes should be repeated in the book as a whole, as well as within the entire body of sacred texts to which it belongs. Thus the first chapter of the first book in the

Bible concerns Adam and Eve and the Tree of Knowledge, while the last chapter of the last book, Revelation, ends with the Spirit, the Bride and the Tree of Life. (1972, pp. 145–6)

The number of glazed circles in the window is 193, which spells 'Iesus Xristos'. In gematria it is allowable to add or subtract the Spirit from the phrase, which is 1. So by this Scarlet would have taken the number 192, which is sixteen times 12. There are 86, or half that number, of cusps in the twelve wheels of the rose, 192 little rosettes carved around the perimeter frame and twice that, or 384, set within the frame itself. And lying within the framing circle of rosettes there are some superb and intricate leaves, and they are not accidental either, but reinforce the original statement. There are 74 of them carved on to 37 stones! Last, each segment of the rose is cut from seven stones, twelve copies of each completing the entire structure. Thus the window is formed from 96 stones, which spells 'Beata Virgo', and if we include the stones in the frame there are 197 which is one more than the Cabalistic subdivisions of the Kingdom of Heaven.

What wouldn't I give to know more about this man!

In the streets adjoining the cathedral there are many doors, perhaps thirty, which have the same detailing and corbels as found in the cathedral. The fire of 1194 devastated much of the town as well as the basilica, for the high wind blew the fire from one house to another until much of the city had been laid waste. It would have been natural for the people to engage the masons working on the cathedral to do the odd pieces of stonework that were needed here and there. Some of this work has survived, as well as a few oddments carved for the church but not used, like a short column now gracing the toilet in one of the houses in Snake Street. This column is identical to Scarlet's work in the spokes of the nave flyers, and must have been carved in 1215.

Similarly with small parish churches, where the gangs from the big contractors may have been deputised to carry out a small addition while the rest of the crew was working on a bigger job. The little church at Lhuys has a small transept that one gang could have built while the rest were working on the near-by abbey church at Braine, and similarly at Santeuil and Gallardon, and St Pierre near Chartres, and again at St Leger in Soissons. If the job did not require everyone's presence, at one stage or another the master could have sent some of them to do small jobs near by. Presumably the foreman would then

101 Detail of the southern rose.

have been in charge, master of his own team. This would explain some of the anomalies found in the doors in Chartres. When measured, the geometry is not always consistent with the work being done under the same corbel in the cathedral. The foreman leading the gang working on the house may at one time have had his own organisation. This raises some interesting questions.

There was a much heavier demand for big builders in the decades around 1200 than there had been before, or was to be after. The teams must have been much smaller in previous decades, and we know from the documents that they were to become smaller later. Our big teams had to grow from the smaller ones either by training new men, importing skilled men from other regions, or by amalgamation. Huge works like Chartres or Reims would have called upon the resources of the largest teams, while for small jobs the big contractor may have merely sub-let the work to one of his component gangs.

If the team had been formed by amalgamation, the sub-groups would naturally have re-formed into the original teams. The

102 The crystalline forms of the north rose.

leadership of the head master may have been lost for a while, and these men would have reverted to the control of their original master, naturally using his design methods rather than those of the man they had been working under. Though we cannot be sure at this stage, they seem to have continued to use the main contractor's corbel and maybe even his foot unit, if not his geometry.

This would help to explain the strong individuality found in many of the gangs, and the influence the foreman had over his men.

Ruby's first program included sculpture and leaves from four gangs, while his second and third campaigns included only three, one of whom had not worked on the first. If that gang was working somewhere else, was its foreman using his own corbels or did he continue to use that of the mother team? Did he use his own foot and geometric ideas, or his master's? If the foreman's techniques were different from those of the contractor, where had he obtained them from, including his foot unit? Why would he carry one foot rather than another, and did the foot mean anything more than a convenient length? This would make the foreman more independent than we have believed. Many questions, and damnably few answers.

It is not impossible that Ruby and Rose, who had very similar corbels, were just different leaders within the one gigantic contracting group, perhaps with other masters on the payroll who did not come to Chartres. They may have had a common pool from which to select the men they needed for each job. Hence the better gangs doing the sculptural work would always have been present in the early years, while in the less demanding upper work the master brought with him only the less skilled gangs. Certainly we find that some of Rose's men begin working under Ruby in the later years. Yet Ruby's detailing is quite unlike Rose's. They use different foot units, one works to harmonics while the other uses pentagons, and so on. Even if they were based on the same quarry and took their gangs from a common pool, the master still ran the job his way.

This suggests a mobility within an already fluid contractual situation that would be even more confusing if it was universal. Fortunately it is not. No other team shows the same internal restlessness as Ruby and Rose. There is one occasion when I feel sure that one of Bronze's gangs did not turn up, but on all other campaigns and with all the other teams the whole group seemed to stay together and worked as a unit on the cathedral. Nevertheless the possibility of some of the contractors being based on a quarry, perhaps among the concentrated group of quarries found around the Oise and the Aisne, is not unreasonable.

In the 1220s and 1230s the Ruby and Rose gangs were even more interchangeable than before. That was when one of the Rose gangs carved the rose windows for the two transepts. No pun is intended here, for I had named this master before I was able to attach the window to him. It was a nice coincidence. The first window in the south was actually installed by Rose but the second, coming from the same shop, was installed by Ruby. There are enough crossed wires between these two teams to suggest a common origin.

If these ideas prove right, it is no wonder that the period has been hard to disentangle. The master seems at times to be like the director of a travelling theatre, where not only will the chief actor take over from time to time, but the stage-sets and the script change as well. How does one find the authors under these conditions?

10
MASTER BRONZE AT WORK: 1201-30

THOUGH THE SITUATION is often fluid and confusing, and though we may never know the names of these masters, we can discover a great deal about them as architects. The clearest ghost to inhabit our stage is Bronze. We can discern the artist in his work, and this is exciting indeed. The curtain of anonymity that has concealed these people from us can be lifted ever so slightly. In the wings real people are waiting.

In 1201 Bronze began the paving stones for the walkway under the sanctuary windows. They were closely butted so that not too much water could work its way between them to infiltrate the wall underneath. Nevertheless Bronze has scooped out the middle of each stone so that the rain would flow towards the centre, and from that he carved small channels to lead it to the outside. He was careful about water, certainly. The detail shows not only his concern, but his belief in his capacity to lead moisture wherever he wanted to.

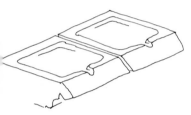

103 The scooped-out centres to the paving slabs Bronze laid to the sanctuary walkway.

Some years later when he was setting out the walls of the choir triforium he did a similar thing. There are two aisles in the sanctuary, which made their roofing more difficult than the single aisle in the nave. Over the inside aisle he decided to repeat the arrangement used in the west where a simple skillion roof covered the attic room behind the triforium arcade. Over the outside aisles he built a series of separate structures made entirely of stone. From the ground they would have imparted a gentle undulation to the silhouette of this level.

So what of the rainwater? From the skillion roof it would flow to where the outside wall would have been if the aisle had been a single one, and from there it had to be taken to the outside. As the outer stone roofs were pyramidical and shed their water in every direction, he was left with only one solution: to run the water between the roofs, so that it flowed along the centre lines of the bays underneath. The water

104 The roof over the southernmost chapels. The supports inside can be seen in Fig. 105. The surrounding gutter is plainly visible.

followed the axes through the piers, and therefore coincided with the idealised routes taken by the loads and thrusts from the whole building. Again Bronze has channelled water meaningfully and with intent.

Few modern architects would have done it this way, for if the water was flowing over the most important parts of the structure there would always be the risk of it leaking and doing some permanent damage. We would be inclined to lead it where there was the least risk. The fact that a competent builder, not unaware of the need to handle water carefully, deliberately led it over the most critical parts of the building indicates that he was guided by other principles.

Digressing for a moment, these pyramidical roofs enclose some of the most wondrous spaces in the building. Yet they do little more than keep the water off the chapel vaults. These rooms were not to be seen

105 The twelve-sided rib vault that supports the stone roof in Fig. 104.

from within the church, for they sit on the filling over the vaults and were therefore built afterwards. And they were not meant to have any particular function, for they contain only old plaster casts and builders' junk. The ribs are set around a 20 foot circle, using Bronze's Teuton foot of 337 mm, and the size of each comes from a hexagonal arrangement placed outside the circle: so if the circle had been larger the ribs would have been bigger too. As the ribs follow a circular curve, the height of the room is half this, and the roofing stones are pitched low. The slabs rest on the large boss at the crown and, at the perimeter where they project beyond the ribs, they are supported on small beams.

These open spandrelled ribs are very exciting. They create an intricate woven pattern within, producing the most stunning lighting effects. They may be the first example in mediaeval architecture of the skeletal rib which was to give such renown to the Bristol and Bohemian masters in later centuries.

The roof is made of finely cut, but irregular shaped, rebated slabs, and the joints between them were set in molten lead. Though some of it needs caulking today to keep out the weather, there has been little deterioration in seven centuries. As long as none of the slabs moves, it is an excellent system, whose permanence is largely due to the size and solidity of the perimeter stones. Some are enormous, the one at the top right corner of the roof in Fig. 104 being 3.5 m long by over half a metre high and must weigh a couple of tons.

106 Roofing stone to the room shown in Figures 104 and 105. The recesses on the underside for the windows are dotted.

This one stone is worth a bit of study. The underside has been rebated for the two windows visible in Fig. 105, or rather for the hinged shutters that were intended to close them. On top there are projections to support decorative gables. At each end there is a special projection to complete the system of rebates and to hold the adjoining stones in place. The edge has a double roll-mould with a groove, and neatly fits against its companions on each side. It is an incredible piece of craftsmanship, particularly when you consider the difficulty of sending all this complex information to the quarry.

The recesses on the underside for the windows were pre-cut before placing the stone, so the walling that supports it must have been placed with care, or more probably the templets for the stone were not cut until the wall under it had been erected. Is this why the average campaign finished no more than three courses of stonework round the building? For until the first course had been cut and placed, the templets for the second could not be prepared. This would mean a delay while the masons were preparing the next row of stones, during which the mortar under the first course would have had time to set.

There is a metal grille across the windows. Its bars are threaded through one another and are let a good 20 mm into the stones at top, bottom and sides. The iron could only have been installed with the stonework itself. It is seven centuries old, and has withstood the weather and rain without rusting for all that time. Mediaeval iron was not as pure as ours, and therefore paradoxically, it lasted longer. Its carbon content was high, and minimised the oxidisation which produces rust. Modern iron would have flaked apart in a few years, and blown out all the stonework around it.

Consider carefully how this stone might have been placed. How do you raise two tons from the workshop floor 20 m below? The best cranes they had were giant 6 m diameter wheels large enough for a number of men to walk round inside. A small drum was attached to the axle, and the rope was passed around this. It may have had an eightfold efficiency. Three hundred steps would be needed to raise any load, even a hundredweight, to the triforium, let alone lift it to the main roof. Theoretically five men walking within the drum would have been enough to raise this giant, but in practice working these wheels is not that simple.

I have used the one at Beverley Minster, and whereas the control can be fingertip precise, there is a real danger of slip. Imagine what would happen if one of the men in the wheel missed his footing, and the steady upward progress of the load was arrested so that the immense weight of the stone was able, all in a moment, to start moving downwards. The wheel would begin to turn the other way, the men inside would be tumbled helter skelter, and it would gather speed with a momentum that nothing could stop. Being bruised and dizzy would be the happiest result, but even then the stone would be smashed as it hit the ground, and all that work would have to be done again.

There were four of these cranes on the job, and one was located on the west side of the second buttress from this roofing slab, alongside the sanctuary wall. Having lifted the monster up to the triforium, ten or more men would have had to grapple it with ropes so that it could be pulled aside and lowered on to the scaffolding. That in itself would not have been too difficult, but think of the sort of scaffolding you would have needed to support this load; and then the difficulties of moving it 10 m horizontally along this platform to its position. After that, it still had to be hoisted up and over the wall, and then settled into place without damaging the work already installed.

We see it finished, with neat edges and tidy joints. The sweat and the blood have been washed away years ago. But go back in time. How do you feel about the layers? How many arms were broken or fingers crushed in erecting these giants? How often did the rope, mere hemp and tar, stretch or snap? And the scaffolding give way? The problems were immense, and were no less for being so far above the ground. They were considerable, these contractors—intrepid, daring and ingenious.

While this room is one of the finest things Bronze did, it does not illustrate his artistic principles. To do that, we must return to structure. At the same time as he was cutting the walkway cornices with the dished centres, he was setting out the big buttress to the east of the sanctuary. We earlier described the design Ruby made for this buttress, but Bronze's part lay under Ruby's and above the cornice over the curved walls of the apse chapels. The centres of these buttresses lie to the east of the axis across the choir, so the forces from the high vaults would, when they came to the outside of the building, have to be bent to one side.

Though the buttress is large, it has been hollowed out for a staircase which creates a weakness right in the middle of the support. Bronze resolved this problem by extending the main cross axis through the wall shaft S into the buttress until it met the curve of the stairwell at A. He then bent it from A through the newell N to the other side B. From B it was continued parallel to the main axis to the epicentre E.

This would have been a perfect buttress if this is the way vectors work in practice. But sadly they do not. They do not go where we place them, but where they will. Failure would have occurred to the left, towards F. The thrust from above would have been restrained by the buttress E on the right and, rotating around A, would have simply folded outwards on the other side. Bronze did not realise this, for he placed no countervailing buttress at F. He thought he only had to arrange a pathway for these thrusts along the most orderly route for them to follow it happily. He was lucky that the building was so over-designed that he was never called to witness the results of such ineptitude.

However, this is not really the right word. Today we are capable of setting up a test and recording the results accurately. They had no way to do that. They could only apply reason, and within the principles he had for handling water he manipulated forces in a similar logical way. He took water by the hand and led it whither he wished, and he did the same with thrusts.

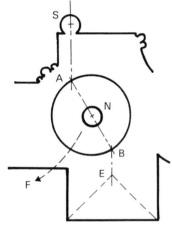

107 Plan of the buttress shown in Fig. 90, at the level of the lower outside 'door'.

The same thinking is shown in the window wall next to this buttress in which he eliminated the solids from the wall and replaced them with thin piers infilled with glass. I said earlier that this arrangement had a modern look about it, in that the functions have been separated from one another, and each stated distinctly and in its own way. The buttresses alone take the load, as do the piers inside, and the master saw that between them he was free to fill in as he wished. The glass wall was Bronze's invention, and shows he was thinking about structure in much the same way as he was thinking about water.

He began with the axis in which both weight and wet could be reduced to a movement along a line. Thin and dimensionless, the line is the most abstract way to delineate a building. Walls, piers and all other masonry is eliminated, and in its place we have a diagram which describes the building quite well enough, but in its essence rather than in its substance.

By reducing architecture to essentials, Bronze gave himself the freedom to re-interpret building form in a totally new way. This is what makes him such an exciting man to study. He did not modify an element from one shape to another just to please the senses. He by-passed this traditional process by re-expressing the elements in their basic forms, and then working outwards from that to the reality of the building.

As a consequence of this innovation, architecture tended over the centuries to become more and more linear. Geometry imperceptibly became formula, where a real event like a mass or a thrust could be made equivalent to a mathematical construct. In a very modern way, reality became abstracted, and the scientific attitude was born. One wonders what part the building of the cathedrals played in hot-housing the ideas that created the modern world view.

From these principles Bronze could see each aspect of a situation in its true nature. Why do we need a wall outside when we only have a pier inside? Why should water simply be allowed to flow anywhere to the detriment of the structure? Why not accept that the string-lines which he had used to set out the building may represent more than just a handy tool, but a truth? It could be similar to the mystic belief that the Essence is most present in the least touchable part of our world, the light, for in Bronze's work the essence of the building could be best expressed in the dimensionless and weightless grid of its axes.

The consequence was one of the most important innovations

108 View from the clerestory walkway of the piers under the flyers, which are semi-octagonal in form at their base.

109 The depth of the rectangle was made one-quarter of the span at this level, and the width is five-sixths of that. The base of the inside triangle was made one-fifth of the bay, and its depth is six-fifths of that. The outside triangle is larger, reflecting the direction of the thrusts. It starts with the same base, but with a depth ratio of 4:3. As a result, by coincidence (?) or intent (!) this depth is equal to the width of the rectangle.

leading to Gothic. When the rib vault was first used in Durham in 1100, even in its pointed form, it was treated with a massiveness that was quite un-Gothic in feeling. Even Bronze's double window could have been adapted to a solid-wall construction. The difference which permeates this period, and which motivated Bronze to the depth of his artistic being, was that the substantiality of stone could be transformed into a pattern of lines, which exalted the abstract above the tangible. The normal process of design was reversed, so that mass and weight were to be secondary to the ethereal web of forces that lay within it.

This feeling that solid stone could be permeated with energy was expressed in the changing forms of the torus moulds described earlier, and in two small but important details in the clerestory buttresses. In the choir the central support under the flyers is semi-octagonal. Bronze's gutters pass through passages within the octagons. The final shape of the octagons come from the combination of two triangles with a rectangle. As you can see in Fig. 109, the masonry occupies the part where both figures overlap. The shape does not follow the extremities of the figure, but is like the envelope that defines common ground.

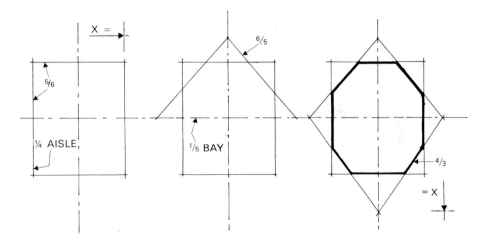

Where the axes are not true to one another, the planes of the octagon are individually twisted to suit them. It is as if the thrust will be taken by the faces of the stonework which must be properly aligned to them if the pier is to withstand the forces on it. It may seem a crazy idea that the face takes the thrust, but if you examine a collapsed building it becomes more reasonable. Afterwards many of the courses that are still standing will be pushed over one another, and it looks as if the

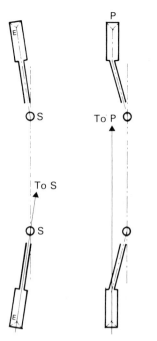

110 Ruby's buttresses are aligned on to the centres of the near-by wall shafts, while Cobalt's, on the right, are twisted off the axis so they are aligned on to the buttress on the other side of the building. How did each of them conceive of the force acting within the building?

surfaces failed to dam the forces inside. The skin is thus more important than the mass in withstanding the side thrusts. It is rather like a bag filled with water where the pressure on the sides can be felt with the hand.

In the nave, most of the axes had been bent from the time of the first plan so that the buttresses and the pier shafts seldom lie on the same line. The first ones put down by Ruby were aligned directly to the centre of the adjoining wall shaft under the vaults. But the next set built by Cobalt were eased over to point towards the buttress on the opposite side of the building. Today we know that the only forces coming on to the buttresses were from the vaults between them, and that there was none from one side of the building across to the other. There could not be, as all thrusts are down and outwards. Yet Cobalt believed there were, otherwise why prepare to receive them?

I get the unmistakable impression that they believed that energy was immanent within the masonry itself, and that these forces were rising as well as descending. This is another expression of the mystic idea in which the Presence is universal and in everything. As these forces were, like light, considered to be high in the hierarchy of things, they were believed to inhabit every part of the building. So by using the right geometric magic they could be pliably adjusted as needed. Thus there was a life which moved within the building, which was not inert stone but, being a cathedral, was also a part of the Divine.

From inside we can still glimpse this today in the fractured prismatic colours of the stained glass that transform the solidity into a shimmer that floats rather than sits. From the outside, too, we get the same message from the projecting flyers which deny the solidity of the enclosure. Everything reinforces the statement that the reality we know is in truth only an illusion. The ultimate reality may be glimpsed in the light around us, and in the energy vibrating within the stones. The masters felt that if they could only tap that, understand it and lead it gently by the right geometric incantations along its apportioned route, they would catch a glimpse into the mystic world of the spirit. They would have made the other world visible from our own. It was all a matter of pattern and number, and of correctly integrating the formulae. It was sympathetic magic, and if it were done rightly, the vision splendid would have to follow.

There were no common incantations, this is the strange thing. Each master seems to have evolved his own, and to have kept his answers to

111 Sainte Modeste in the
north porch, by a member of
the Bronze crew.

himself. Similarly there were no conferences between the clergy who communed with God and the masters who daily strove to extract his Essence in stone. The two disciplines strayed along different paths. Nowhere in the enormous fund of clerical literature do we find any appreciation for the builder's grotesque yet inspired struggle with all this magic. Nor do we find one master sharing his ideas with another. There is no agreed procedure, and few common rules. Even Scarlet's extraordinary plan for the cathedral received little sympathy from his successors. It was just by-passed and another squeezed into its place.

Such individualism in an age which believed in the corporate piety of the church may seem strange until we remember that it was also the age of Norman barons in search of plunder, of Venetian merchants diverting the Crusades to their own ignoble purposes, and of the most incredible variety of pilgrimages, markets and fairs, of petty princedoms and of religious ideas both catholic and heretical. The middle ages was a much more individualistic and venturesome time than most primitive and many historical cultures. This free energy was combined for a short but brilliant period in the twelfth century with a profound other-worldliness and mysticism which steered every citizen, in his own personal way, towards a vision of the spirit.

Bronze's own approach to the ebb and flow of these immaterial forces can be seen in his sculpture. Examine the figure of Modeste in the north porch, or the angels in the south. How liquid is the cloth, flowing like the finest silk through her soft fingers. See how it tumbles free and relaxed at her feet. This cloth is amazing. It is pure light, rippling and gliding by its own laws: not by the body it covers, but to please itself. Other figures by his men, such as Judith and Joseph in the Job doorway, and some of the priests near by, show the same qualities.

Just compare them to Ruby's massive Abraham and Isaac. These sculptures are equally individual and sensitive, but are indubitably made of stone. Their solid bodies direct their clothing. They are not muscle men, but just weighty, like Ruby's nave walls and the single windows he thrust through them. Where Ruby is a mason with a quarryman's sense of solidity, Bronze is a dreamer, happier with a compass than with a chisel.

Bronze's drive to find an essence within the stone, which would avoid its weightiness while still expressing all its needs and functions, can be seen in the way he evolved his windows. This one (Fig. 113), set into a corner over the southern porch, was the very devil to measure,

112 Abraham by the Ruby 'Forker' gang in the north central door.

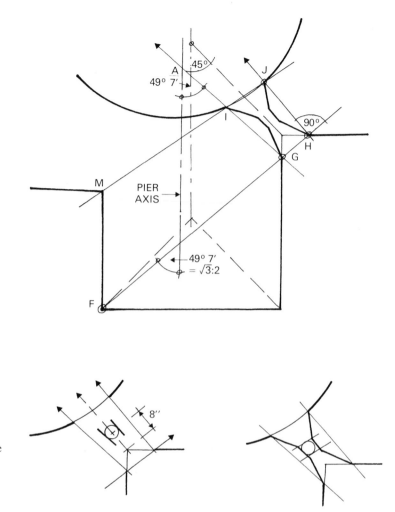

113 Bronze's window out of
the stairs above the southern
porch roof. The sketches at the
bottom show the circles and
tangents which form the inner
box.

for the sides are irregular and it was not easy to locate the staircase
inside in relation to the sides of the buttress outside.

After the golden mean, Bronze's favourite ratio was $2 : \sqrt{3}$, formed
from the side and the vertical of an equilateral triangle. He used this
ratio to form the inclination of the line from the corner of the buttress
F. This line intersected the corner between the buttress and the wall
at G and H. He used the same ratio for the line back from G to the
axis at A. Both these angles were measured from the axis which reflects
the line of the arcade piers inside the transept.

From H he drew the line perpendicular to FG, to where it cut the curve of the stairwell at J. This box GHIJ locates all four of the external corners of the window. The centre was formed by equally geometric steps through a circle with another box set round it whose sides lay parallel to the adjoining sides of the outer box. To make the window from this, all he had to do was to join the corners.

The stairwell and the buttress were not of Bronze's making, so he could not have intended to use this $2:\sqrt{3}$ at the time the buttress was set out. I imagine when he came to this part he had string-lines placed along the axes and, standing on the partly built buttress itself, tried to visualise the best way to design the window. Today we would have taken it back to the drawing board, for it is not easy for modern architects to design *in situ*. But, by standing on the spot, he saw the possibilities of using the corner F. No doubt he had a feeling for the size of window he wanted and had to search for an appropriate formula. As Bronze used a number of starting points and different ratios in his other windows he doubtless followed the Biblical injunction to 'seek, and ye shall find'. However, in every one of his windows from this time onwards the basic technique is always the same: form a box whose corners may be joined to form the sides.

I feel this approach has the same characteristics as his window walls. The surface that defines the mass is secondary, while the points, which are as dimensionless as the axes, determined the form.

There is usually a validation process in all mediaeval geometry. For how would you as a creative geometer know, with as much certainty as possible, that your arrangement is the truest one? I use this word rather than 'best' for it suggests something beyond personal preference, while the other is merely competitive. 'Truth' in geometry can be expressed as a harmony where all the parts merge into a unity. Bronze found it in this case when, after working on the problem, he saw that he could extend the last side of the box JI to the left so that it would meet the internal corner of the buttress at M. There is a similar validation in the Creation Figure and in the octagonal pier discussed earlier, in the two 'X' dimensions shown in Fig. 109.

I think Bronze began the geometry from F, as there is a geometric relationship between FG and the pier axis, while there is none between JM and any other part. This last line just closes the circle, and in the process satisfied the artist in him. In a way this sort of circularity was like a proof of God's presence. The geometry returns on itself and shows that he had it right. Returning to the beginning may have been the mediaeval equivalent of today's scientific method.

We are lucky at Chartres, for we can show how a master came to evolve one of his design concepts. It is a rare privilege, for normally we have only the finished product to look at, and the steps in between have melted away along with the drawings and the master who made them.

The two transept porches are identical and symmetrical. The four staircases inside them look out of similar windows set within the reveals between the doorways, one of which is shown in Fig. 25. The archaeological evidence shows that the south-east one was set out first, followed by the south-west, the north-west and lastly the north-east.

All were built within the one campaign of 1198.

See how the form of the first is fairly simple, half the reveal in width, and made from a mechanical arrangement of 45° triangles. In the next

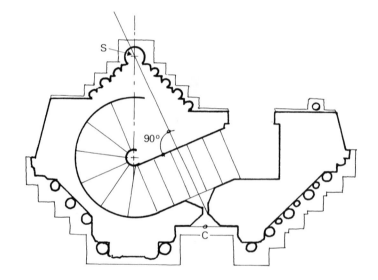

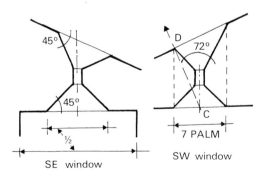

114 The 'almost' box in the south-west window became an exact one in the two north windows, and their centres were derived from the shaft S, unlike those in the south.

he must have felt dissatisfied with the balance of the south-west one, for he reduced the size of the outer triangle, used a golden mean triangle inside, and saw to it that the slot occupied the central part of the wall. Maybe Bronze had been preoccupied with client meetings or labour troubles when he did the first window, for the second one has a much pleasanter feel, both in plan and from the outside. In it he was also able to draw the line from the middle of the outside triangle, true to the inside wall, and saw that it passed through the corner D of the inner splays.

This was the critical moment. The window was becoming more integrated, and the inside triangle had been located from the point D rather than from the plane of the wall. It was then that he could have noticed that the window had almost fitted between two parallel lines, shown dotted in Fig. 114. Suddenly he was struck with the possibility of working to corners rather than to planes. The thought felt good to him. It touched the artist and resonated. The surfaces would then become less important, while the point was beginning to take its place. It was like designing the wall from the axis, as he was able to do in the sanctuary window walls three years later. So in the third window he formed a box, geometrically of course, placed a 45° triangle outside, a pentagonal triangle inside, and the usual slot in the middle.

His second great discovery was to see that the window could be integrated with the structure as well as with the wall in which it sat. The line which joined CD in the second window still appeared in the third, but this time he saw that if he extended it into the interior it would pass through the centre of the wall shaft S. The minor element could now be located from the greater. The window was no longer a self-contained form within the wall, even if it had been located in the centre of the panel, but an expression of an inner and thus more essential function. Bronze saw at once that the shaft was the major item, and the window the minor, and that the window should therefore be dependant on the other, even if the result looked a little weird.

For this is what happened in the last window, the north-west. On this side the relationship between the shaft and the reveal was a little different from the others, so that, by setting out the window from the shaft, the centre no longer fell in the middle of the reveal. He could now accept the correctness of this move, for though the observer may have seen something strange, here was a truth that lay behind the obvious. It is in this last window that we see the first statement of the new Bronze. He must have hugged himself as the impact of where he was going dawned on him. The process was good now, from the axes of the inner structure to the box, then to the corners and lastly to the planes.

But can we explain why these changes were taking place? Had the three great doorways been laid out by the leader of the team? For their geometry is incomparably magnificent, though not based on corners. And were the windows left to his assistant? Or did the master, after setting out the porch, leave town to supervise another job so that his understudy had to do the windows? Or does this indicate a change in the crew's leadership some time in 1198? Had the old master died?

Whatever happened during this campaign, by the time the crew returned in 1201 the second man was in complete charge. All the slot windows were being designed from the corners. The old master had left permanently, and the crew had a new boss. He was still master in 1230 when the windows at the top of the northern apsidal tower were laid out, for the technique is essentially identical to the one he had evolved in the doorways thirty-two years earlier. This is a long time for one man to lead a team, but not too unreasonable. Had he taken over in his early thirties he would still have been in control in his mid-sixties.

He must have received much of his training under his predecessor, for when he took over he continued to use the same corbel (though he reduced its size), the same foot unit and square, and the same proportional ratios of $2:\sqrt{3}$ and the golden mean. The plinths do not change, nor do the tori under the columns, nor the leaves. As these may have been left to the leading hands, there would inevitably have been a permanence in these individualistic statements. But there is an overriding continuity within these contractors that lasts not just for decades, but for centuries. I have found evidence for one crew working in different parts of the area from the mid-1100s to almost 1400, maintaining something constant in spite of the dozen masters who could have led them over those years.

There must have been some loyalty to the institution as such, for otherwise there would be greater changes of ideas and personnel when one leader was succeeded by another. Perhaps it was like men's devotion to the church and to the royal family in spite of the inadequacies of individual popes and kings. So when we speak of the masters of the great cathedrals we speak equally of the organisations they led. No pope can be understood in isolation from the church he

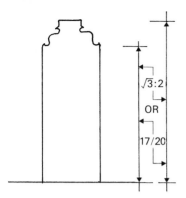

115 Bronze's corbel geometry.

rules, nor can a king's actions be understood without some sense of the interplay of passion and greed that surrounds power. The masters may have been feudal chieftains leading their men into the fray, but they were as influenced by their men as any pope or king.

Some masters permitted a greater freedom to their masons, and others were more authoritarian. Scarlet ran the whole ship, well trimmed and to his precise commands. Olive and Bronze were more relaxed. Bronze issued a general directive that corbels were to be arranged within the opening using the $2:\sqrt{3}$ ratio, and on the whole they were. But in a few corbels, seemingly the work of one gang in particular, a numerical approximation was used for this ratio of 20:17. It meant that the foreman only had to measure the height of the opening, divide it into twentieths, and use three of these for the height of the corbel.

A similar thing can be observed in the bosses. All those in the nave aisles follow the same flat and radial pattern. Simple pancake-like leaves are laid over the boss, and the arrangement in one quadrant is exactly matched in the next. Fifteen bosses were carved by the one gang, and though at least five men were involved in the cutting, the foreman imposed his own will on them, and insisted they follow the same unfortunate and uninspired arrangement.

These were put up at the beginning of the campaign of 1205. Near the end, just before Bronze took his men away—possibly in the direction of Braine—he had four bosses carved in the sanctuary. They have none of the uniformity found in the nave. Each is an individual design, with a rich surface texture and a busy intricate patterning never to be found in the nave. Each boss is different, not only in the design, but the geometry used. Some have eight leaves within four, some a fourfold cluster of branches and berries, and one has sixteen leaves twisted and swirling in the one clockwise direction.

What were the master's directions to his men? Why did he permit both the uniformity of the nave and the idiosyncrasy of the choir? What made him choose the authoritarian gang for the former, and not choose him again for the others? He must have known how differently he would have handled the problem. Or were there boundaries to the master's authority beyond which he either learned or did not wish to concern himself? It is rare to find the answer to one question that does not open up a lot more.

There is one other item in which we can see Bronze's creative

188 · CHARTRES

powers at work. Again it has to do with water. The copings over the flyers normally shed the water to either side, like those in the nave, or the lower ones in the choir. But over the upper eastern arches, Bronze introduced a new moulding which, as we would expect, leads the water towards the outside. It does not just shed it on to the roofs below, but directs it along the lines of the axes away from the building.

I have found a number of these mouldings in France, and they follow an orderly progression. The simplest and possibly therefore the earliest is in the north-east corner flyer of the impressive abbey church at Orbais. The one at Chartres is rather more appropriately detailed to channel the water, and, where the coping meets the tower, there is a gutter to lead the water to one side. Here he has shown a greater awareness of the way water is being moved, and is trying to resolve the problems of distribution better than in the copings over the lower arch of the flyers of St Pierre near by which just butt into the back of the buttress. Chartres is dated 1222.

However, the same coping has been used in the small church of Gallardon only a few miles north of Chartres. Here the water runs down the gutter and at the buttress passes through a channel to be thrown clear of the building through gargoyles. Was this the first use of this famous detail? Bronze had earlier used projecting spouts carved as leonine heads to dispel the water over the south porch in 1205. Did it take another seventeen years to apply this to buttresses and flyers? I would not be surprised, for ideas changed slowly, and architects seemed to proceed step by step from one creative idea to the next, each firmly built upon the proven worth of the ones before.

But Bronze did not stop there. In the uppermost flyers at St Pierre he proceeded one step further. He applied the idea he had used in the paving stones of the sanctuary walkway, but instead of scooping out each one to keep the water away from the joint, he formed them into channels that led the water from the main roof towards each flyer. It then ran along the top of the coping to be discharged clear of the building through the cantilevered gargoyles. Bronze has here eliminated a dangerous problem, of the endless and recurrent flow of water over the triforium roofs from the main roof. Every time it rained, the water fell in great gushes from one level to the other, constantly wearing and seeking out the weaknesses in the lower roofs and gutters. Certainly not good for a building. It was like having to withstand the jet of a fireman's hose for centuries.

116 Copings to the upper flyers in the choir.

Bronze's device, tentative as it was at St Pierre, was excellent. It collected the upper water and took it away, completely clear of the building. Here is an orderly progression of ideas that grew from a quirk into a solid invention of the highest order. It became in later years a standard solution and there is hardly a Gothic building with flyers that does not use the upper arch to lead away the water.

But this is not just a matter of water, but of guidance. Bronze has not blocked it off, or carried it away in hidden downpipes, but conducted it gently towards the safest disposal points. The axis still represented the essence of the building, for everything was amalgamated with it. And between lie the infill spaces occupied by roofs rather than gutters, and glass rather than structure. We could perhaps call Bronze the man who exemplified the phrase 'form follows the essence'. He was one of the most formative and original men of the period, audacious in his ideas, strangely twentieth-century in his thinking, who over a long life introduced into French architecture some of the most sublime concepts that were to enhance the work of many future generations.

I have found the discovery of these men the most exciting part of my work. To glimpse real people among the ghosts of a period gives it life and vitality. They worked in a way that we of the twentieth century would find hard to emulate, for we have neither their faith nor their geometry, and certainly not their essential simplicity. Without their certainty that God would see that his work was done, I doubt that we would undertake these projects in the first place, let alone entrust them to such a diverse cavalcade of masters. And without their geometry and the depth and unity this engendered we could have made a hash of it, even if we could have started.

The great cathedrals, and the multitude of abbeys and castles, are entirely and solely a product of the middle ages. The outstanding qualities of these people were their audacity and their trust, their sense of tradition and their sensitivity to the work of others.

They accepted, and indeed made a virtue of the fact, that building was more of a process than a project. It was a natural growth which took a generation or more to evolve into its final form. Chartres is an accumulation of historic events set in stone. It is an organism that evolved towards a common image of the Heavenly City, and that reflects something of each man's vision as well.

GLOSSARY

aedicule	The temple-like terminations to the choir buttresses with gables supported on close-set columns.
aisle	The side passage which surrounds the main vessel of the church.
ambulatory	The extension of the aisles round the curve of the apse.
apse	The eastern complex of the church, with all the parts within the curved section including ambulatory, chapels and rondpoint.
arcade	The range of arches supported on piers which separates the aisle from the main space. Also a smaller range as in the triforium.
axis	The imaginary straight lines around which the work or its elements are arranged symmetrically.
bay	A spacial division down the length of the building, which divides it into sections from the floor to the roof. The piers mark the division between each bay. See Span.
boss	The keystone of the vault where the ribs intersect, at Chartres they are sculptured and are pierced with a round hole.
capital	The carved stone which caps a column or pier, and which forms the transition between the shape of the column and the arches over it.
cell	The curved infill between the ribs of the vault.
centering	The temporary framework on which arches and ribs are supported while they are being put together.
choir	The eastern end of the church from the crossing to the apse.
clerestory	The third storey of the building with big windows, above the aisles and triforium.
corbel	A projection out of a wall to support a lintel, a column or a rib. Here often carved in a characteristic way by each crew.
cornice	Large projecting decorated moulding that runs horizontally around the outside of the building, designed to throw the rain water clear of the face of the wall underneath.

embrasure	The angled side walls to the doorways, where the wall figures are placed.
epicentre	The design centre within the mass of a buttress, from which the geometry of the element is taken.
flyer and flying buttress	Where the high vaults meet the wall of the clerestory, the side thrust is carried to the outside buttresses of the building by an arch, or a group of arches. They span over the roof of the aisle.
jubé	The carved screen which separated the crossing from the sanctuary until it was demolished in 1763.
lintel	The stone which forms the head or top of a door, usually here supported on corbels. Also the horizontal stone beams across the porch which hold up its vault.
nave	The central vessel of the church, between the aisles and under the high vaults. Used here for the western half of the building.
newell	The column which supports the centre of the circular staircases.
ostium	Sentry-box-like recess in the buttresses of the nave above the triforium.
pier	The compound columns supporting the arcades down each side of the main vessel, called by the French *pilier cantonné*. Also the outer supports to the porch vaults.
porch	The covered projecting structures in front of the transept doorways, including the lintels, the vaults over them, and the outside piers which support them.
rib	The arch used to support the vault set diagonally to the bay, where the arch which is square to the bay is called the transverse arch.
rondpoint	The curved eastern end of the main vessel of the church, separating it from the ambulatory. It is the innermost part of the apse, and includes the piers set on its curve.
sanctuary	The straight eastern section of the cathedral, consisting of the four bays to the east of the crossing.
scotia and torus	Circular mouldings that cover the transformation of the column from the square base or plinth. The scotia is concave and is framed by two convex tori.
sill	The stone which frames the underside of a window, sometimes only slightly pitched as in the clerestory, and sometimes steeply sloping as in the nave aisles.
span	The spatial division across the building which separates one arcade from another. It is perpendicular to the bay.

spokes	The radiating columns which separate the two lower arches of the flyers, here set on the radius of the arch curves.
springing	The level from which the arch begins to curve inwards from its support. Usually over the capital.
templet	The full-size outline of a moulding or element, usually cut from thin pieces of wood, to the design prepared by the master mason himself, and then issued to the carvers who prepare the stones themselves.
triforium	The passage on the first floor that covers the roof over the aisles. It is screened from the nave by an arcade of columns.
tympanum	The space between the lintel over a doorway and the arch that rises over that, as in the transepts where they are carved.
vault	Arched masonry ceilings where the different parts of the curved stonework lean against each other for support. The side thrusts produced must be taken either by thick walls, buttresses or flyers.

BIBLIOGRAPHY

BRANNER, R., *Chartres Cathedral*, Norton, New York, 1969.

CONANT, K. J.., 'Medieval Academy excavations at Cluny: IX', *Speculum*, 38, 1963.

HARVEY, J., *The Medieval Architect*, Wayland, London, 1972.

HENDERSON, G. D. S., *Chartres*, Penguin Books, 1968.

HESSE, H., *The Glass Bead Game*, Cape, London, 1972.

JAMES, J., *The Contractors of Chartres*, 2 vols, Mandorla Publications, Wyong, NSW, 1979, 1981.

KATZENELLENBOGEN, A., *The Sculptural Programs of Chartres Cathedral*, Johns Hopkins Press, 1959.

MEULEN, J. VAN DER, 'Recent literature on the chronology of Chartres Cathedral', *Art Bulletin*, 1967, pp. 152–72.

MICHELL, J., *The City of Revelation*, Garnstone Press, London, 1972.

MURRAY, S., 'The completion of the nave of Troyes Cathedral', *Journal of the Society of Architectural Historians*, 1975, pp. 121–39.

PANOFSKY, E., *Gothic Architecture and Scholasticism*, Archabbey Press, Latrobe, Pa., 1951.

SHELBY, L. R., 'The mathematical knowledge of medieval architects', *Journal of the Society of Architectural Historians*, 1971, p. 238.

SIMSON, O. VON, *The Gothic Cathedral*, Princeton University Press, 1964.

ACKNOWLEDGMENTS

Figures 1, 3 and 53 © Caisse National des Monuments Historiques et des Sites and SPADEM, Paris, 1981.
Figure 84 is reproduced by courtesy of the Royal Institute of British Architects.
Figures 2 and 9 appeared in Lassus and Durand, *Monographie de la Cathédrale de Chartres*, Paris, 1842–65.

INDEX

epicentres, 95, 110, 193
Essomes, abbey of St Ferréol, 20
evolution of ideas, 63, 141, 184, 189f

fires: (1194), 5, 21, 51f, 60, 63, 80,
    165; (1836) 3, 63
floor and paving, *see* labyrinth
flyers, spokes and gussets, 5, 4, 15f,
    10, **11**, 47f, **35**, 63, 71, 77f, **77**, **78**,
    122, **108**, 110, 116, 193; copings,
    189f
foot units and rules, 37, 38, 40f, 47,
    63, 94, 96, 103, 105, 148f, **93**, 167,
    171, 186
forces and thrusts, 5f, 31, 119, 153f,
    174, 177f, **110**; wind loads, 32
foremen, *see* organisation
formwork, scaffolding and centering,
    41, 49, 61, 68, 77, 155, 160, 163,
    192
foundations, footings, 32, 56, 80, 91,
    62, 100, 114, 154

gables, 26, 78, 131
Gallardon, St Pierre, 144, 165, 189
gangs, *see* organisation
gargoyles, *see* drains
Gaucher de Reims, 133
gematria, 106f, **66**, 164f; *see also*
    meaning
geometry 32f, 34f, 38f, 63, 74, 94f,
    99f, 103, 105, 114f, **83**, **84**, 147,
    149f, 159f, 163, 175, **109**, 177,
    187; more important than
    aesthetics, 102f, 147f, 154f;
    separate systems, 163; setting-out
    techniques, 116, 155f; solid
    geometry, 155f; *see also* dialectics;
Gil de Hotendon, 34   [meaning
glass wall, 46, 62, 66, 175
golden mean, 114, **71**, 157, **96**, **97**,
    159f, 185
Green, master mason, **18**
gutters, *see* drains

hexagons, 96f, **59**, 99f, 110, **68**

impost, 30, **96**
individuality of masters and men,
    23–50, 105, 122, 141, 143, 169–90
iron, 29, 172
irrational $\sqrt{2}$ and $\sqrt{3}$, 32f, 39, 98,
    114, 116, 183

Jade, master mason, **18**

Jean d'Orbais, 133
Jean le Loup, 133
jubé and stalls, 3, 61, 81, 193

labyrinth and floor, 80, 81, 86f, **51**,
    52, 93f, 102, 110, 130, 132f, 153,
    156
Lagny, Notre-Dame des Ardents,
    30, 130
Laon Cathedral, 20, 62, 63, 75, 130,
    144
Le Mans Cathedral, 63
Lhuys, SS Medard-Gildard, 165
limestone: types and working, 1, 24,
    82, 143; ways of cutting, 27, 29,
    31
Limoges Cathedral, 126
lintels, 36f, 57, 59, 68f, 141, 193
Louis, Count of Chartres, 60, 83,
    137
Louis, Count of Vendôme, 79
Luzarches, church, 132

maintenance men, *see* architect
mason's marks, 24f, **16**, 73
masters, 3f, 7, 13, 21, 23–50, 116f;
    artistic personalities and building
    philosophies, **18**, 28, 31f, 38, 40,
    83–112, 114, 117f, 153, 169–90;
    changes in methods; 63, 141, 184;
    see also individual masters
masters and predecessors' decisions,
    23–50, 46f, 71, 104f, 117, 125f,
    145f, 156, 159, 163f; not touching
    stones in place, 125, 146;
    tradition and that of clergy, 104,
    110, 116f, 178f; *see also*
    contracting
meaning, significance, sacral
    tradition, 33f, 66f, 83–112, 116,
    149, 153f, 156f, 160f, 163, 175,
    178; left *v.* right, 90; *see also*
    gematria; geometry; number
measuring, 24, 28, 31, 35f, 149
mobility of teams, *see* contracting,
    discontinuous
models, 31, 71f, 73
modules and rods, 98, **87**, 155f, 159,
    160, **98**; taken from site, not from
    drawings, 159f
money, income and costs, 43, 49, 62,
    77, 124f, 133, 136f, 139; today's
    cost, 133f
mortar, 24, 32, 41f, 57, 172

narthex 3, 79, **50**, 92
nave, 9f, 46, 62, 71, 73, 85f, 95, **58**,
    77, 78, 157f, 187, 193; squashed
    bays at west, 19, 117
Noyon Cathedral, 20
number, 84f, 87f, 94, 96, 101f, 103,
    105f, 111, 156, 164f; *see also*
    gematria; meaning

Olive, master mason, 24f, **16**, **17**, **18**,
    27f, **19**, **20**, 22, 31, **23**, 46, 73,
    116, **74**, 117, **75**, 129, 141, 187
opinions held by scholars, 52, 123;
    bay-by-bay construction, 21; east
    or west first, 13, 17, 24f;
    permanent workshops, 127, 130;
    sculpture and porches, 56f; *see
    also* construction
Orbais, abbey of St Pierre, 20, 189
organ, 3, 78f, 80f
organisation of builders on site,
    quarries, gangs, foremen, varieties
    of contract, 33, 43, 50, 65, 133f,
    140f, 165, 168
ostium, 77, 122, 193

Paris, Notre-Dame, 1, 20, 56f, 129,
    141
payments to masons, 24, 139
Philippe-Auguste, king, 53, 56, 60f
Philippe le Breton, 53f
Pierre de Roissy, 69f
piers, *see* shafts
pilasters, *see* buttresses
plaster, 82
plinths, tori, 28f, 31, 117, **75**, 122,
    129, 142f, **82**, 193
porches, 8, **18**, **12**, **13**, **35**, **34**, 57f,
    38–**41**, 60f, 80, 180, 193
previous cathedrals at Chartres, 5,
    52, 55f, 91

quality of workmanship and
    accuracy, 24, 78, 116, 143, 154,
    172f

Red, master mason, **18**
Regnault de Cormant, 130
Reims Cathedral, 1, 46, 75, 129,
    130, 133, 136, 166
repairs, redesign, reconstruction and
    demolition, 1, 61, 71, 75f, 78f,
    81f, 91
ribs, *see* vaults